GENESIS UNZIPPED

LUCIO LICCIARDELLO

Speculative theory on the creation of our solar system, Earth, and its inhabitants.

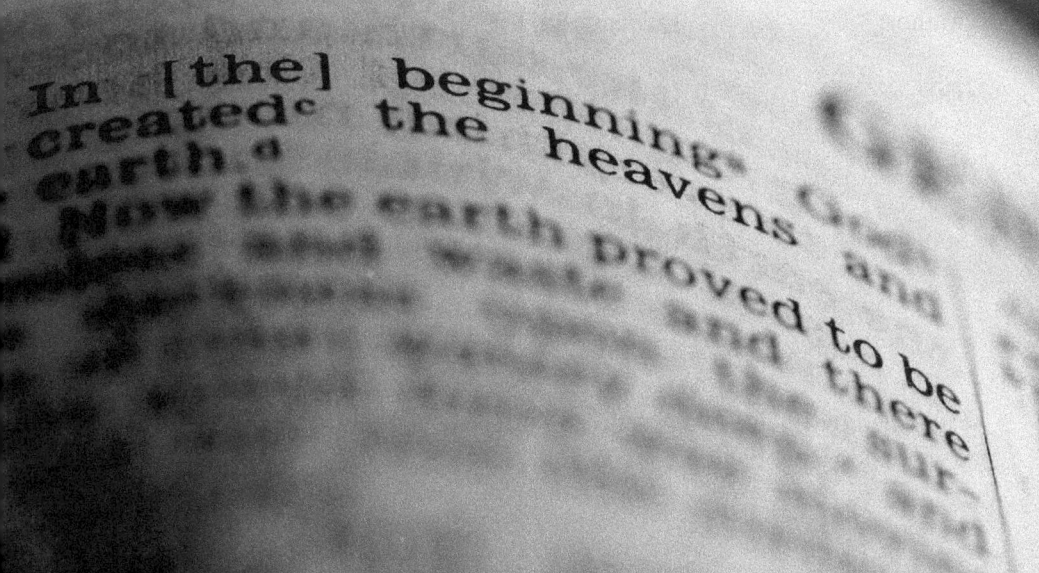

Genesis unzipped
© Lucio Licciardello 2015

All rights reserved. No part of this publication may be reproduced, stored in a retrieval system, or transmitted in any form or by any means, electronic, mechanical, photocopying, recording or otherwise, without the prior written permission of the author.

National Library of Australia Cataloguing-in-Publication entry

Author:	Licciardello, Lucio, author.
Title:	Genesis unzipped / Lucio Licciardello.
ISBN:	9780994236104 (paperback)
Subjects:	Bible. Genesis--Commentaries.
	Bible. Genesis--Criticism, interpretation, etc.
Dewey Number:	222.11

Published by Lucio Licciardello and InHouse Publishing
www.inhousepublishing.com.au

Contents

Part 1 5

Part 2 31

CHAPTER ONE: In the Beginning 33

CHAPTER TWO: Planet X 41

CHAPTER THREE: Creation 49

CHAPTER FOUR: There Were Giants in the Earth 61

CHAPTER FIVE: And, Behold, I, Even I,
Do Bring a Flood of Waters Upon the Earth 67

CHAPTER SIX: Stairway to Heaven 73

CHAPTER SEVEN: The Beginning of Time 75

CHAPTER EIGHT: Babylon, Sodom and Gomorrah 83

CHAPTER NINE: The One God 89

CHAPTER TEN: A Universal Language 91

CHAPTER ELEVEN: What's in a Name? 101

CHAPTER TWELVE: Some Questions Answered by the Stars 111

Bibliography 117

Part 1

In the world of today a zip file format is used to compress information for sending through the internet. When unzipped at its destination the full file is downloaded in a format we can process. In a similar fashion, *Genesis Unzipped* will attempt to unlock the Book of Genesis with an extended theoretical recreation, that looks for answers to questions, and an insight into the full story.

I first heard of the Book of Genesis many years ago at school during scripture lessons. At that time I was taught that God made Earth, including mankind, in seven days. I was taught that in 1650, in his book titled *The Annals of the World,* Archbishop James Ussher, using information found in the Book of Genesis, claimed to have calculated the age of the earth to be around 6,000 years old. A contradiction to this teaching soon arose during a science lesson when we were taught that Earth itself was 4.5 billion years old with life appearing suddenly 3.5 billion years ago. This seemed to disprove what we were taught in scripture. What science could not explain, however, was how life suddenly appeared, or the sudden appearance of our own species, homo sapiens.

The theory of evolution seemed to explain up to the primate homo erectus, but there was a missing link in the evolution between homo erectus and modern humans. The time period between homo erectus and homo sapiens was too short to allow evolution to take place. The truth was that homo sapiens had no evolutionary predecessors. This seemed to prove the biblical story about man being created by God, since science could supply no better answer. Subsequently, since there was truth in both the science and scripture I learned at school, I chose to believe both. In 1969 Erich von Daniken told the world his Ancient Astronaut Hypothesis in a television documentary and a book called *Chariots of the Gods*. This created more possibilities and only added to the confusion.

The subject of Earth's origin and ancient people has interested me ever since. In the years that followed, doing my own research, I have discovered that not only did homo sapiens appear suddenly, but the most ancient people seemed to be the most intelligent. In many ways people of today have not caught up with the technology possessed by ancient people. Many scholars agree that today people could not build another structure identical to the pyramids of Giza. The pyramids of Giza are some of the most famous of ancient artefacts. There are thousands of ancient ruins and monuments all over the world that defy explanation by modern standards.

The city of Cusco in Peru is well known for being the capital of the ancient Inca Empire. One of the most notable features of Inca architecture is their widespread use of large, tightly fitting stones, some weighing over 100 tonnes. These massive stones were cut and fitted together so precisely that not even a razor blade can fit between the joints. The structures were made by cutting and fitting together odd-shaped stones, like they were putting together a giant 3D jigsaw puzzle. Some of the odd-shaped stones had up to twelve sides.

It is still not known how Cusco was built or how its stones were quarried. It has been suggested that to achieve the tight fit, the stones would have been heated to an extremely high temperature, then stacked together while still molten. This would have allowed the stones to fuse together perfectly, without the use of any mortar. If this method of construction proves correct, then the Incas possessed technology that we do not have today.

When the Spanish of 1533 conquered Cusco Peru, they destroyed much of the Inca stonework and reused the stone to build their own structures. Ironically, in 1950 during a major earthquake, the Spanish buildings fell down while the unmortared Inca stoneworks survived intact.

Speaking for myself, I've been involved in the engraving industry for over thirty years. During this time I've seen many technical advances and computer science is constantly improving the precision with which we can engrave. Even with our 21st century technology, compared to some of the work done by ancient people, they remain not only competitive but in many ways the quality and the magnitude of the scale of their work makes us look primitive. At one ancient site called Mada'in Saleh in Saudi Arabia, the gigantic 5,000 year old tombs have been precisely carved into existing stone. This appears to be an impossible task by any standards, yet the site features 131 monumental rock-cut tombs.

A recent documentary series on the History Channel, *Ancient Aliens*, demonstrates the complexity of ancient engineering at a temple complex known as Puma Punku at Tiwanaku Bolivia. At Puma Punku there were enough of the remains left for archaeologists to reconstruct the method used for building. What they found was amazing. Puma Punku was made of giant stone blocks, some weighing up to 131 metric tons. The blocks had been precisely cut into interlocking shapes that were identical to each other. With this method, the stone blocks would slide into place locking them, without the use of any mortar. Plus, the blocks being identical allowed the builders to change the layout of the building as they pleased.

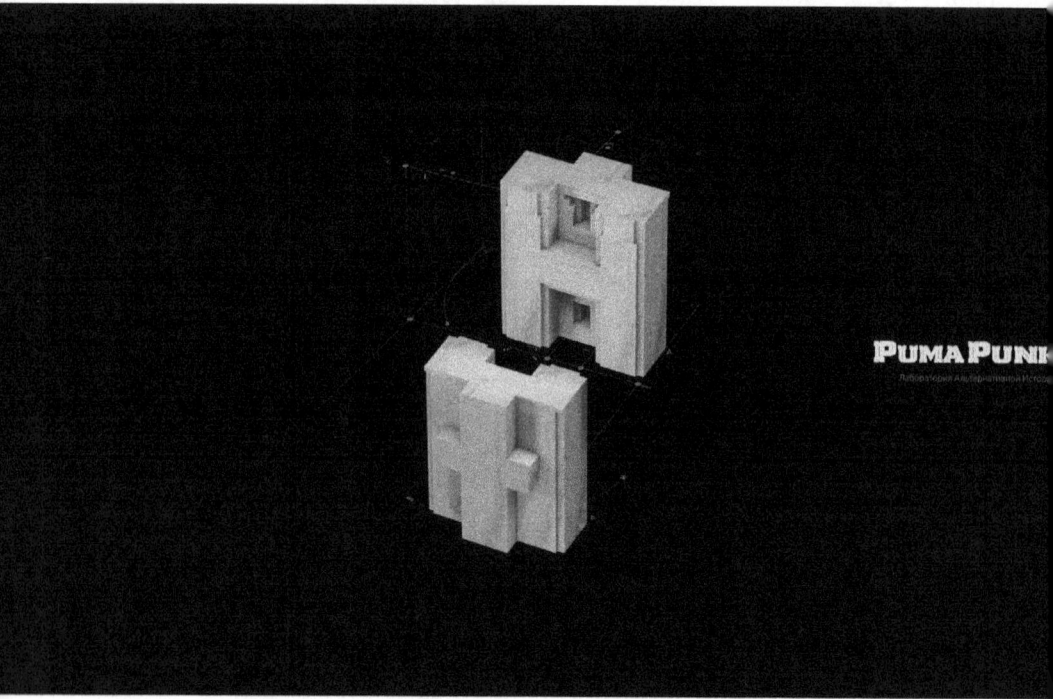

To obtain such precision while cutting into stone, the only possible way it could have been achieved was to use a giant rotary saw studded with diamonds. To construct a giant cutting wheel encrusted with diamonds today would cost millions of dollars in diamonds alone. It is difficult to know how much diamonds cost at the time Puma Punku was built, but it's fair to say that the huge amount of diamonds needed is a very good indication of the affluence of their society.

Very little is known of the people who built Puma Punku. Their dissappearance was as sudden as their appearance, however they did leave one clue. The strange wedge-shaped writing found at Puma Punku looks mysteriously like the cuneiform script of the Sumerians.

The Sumerian civilisation was the most ancient ever found on Earth. Predating even the Egyptians, the Sumerians seem to be the first for everything. They gave us the first multi-storey skyscrapers, the first wheels, the first metalwork, the first money, the first writing, the first engraving, the first medicine. In fact, they had all the basic components that we take for granted in our society today. There is no evidence however that there was ever a time when they did not have all of these things. They appeared suddenly as a complete and highly advanced civilisation. Their knowledge did not evolve, it was something they always possessed, and as a rule their knowledge was not passed on either. Most of what we have learned about the Sumerians today comes from discoveries in the ruins of ancient cities such as the city of Ur.

In fact we are not only learning about the Sumerians, we are still learning from them. Thought to have originated in Ur 5,700 years ago, the discovery of the lost-wax casting process highlights this point.

The lost-wax casting process is used to make moulds for casting metal figurines and statues using beeswax. The figure is sculptured out of beeswax. The wax sculpture is then covered in clay and fired in a kiln. While the clay turnes to stone the wax melts leaving a hollow stone mould which is then filled with a molten metal like gold, silver or bronze. When the metal cools the stone is broken away leaving a perfect golden or metal replica of the original beeswax sculpture.

What is interesting here is that this method of casting was not in use until the discovery was made, hence the name "lost-wax casting". Today this method is widely used in foundaries around the world and is known as "investment casting". The question we need to ask ourselves here is, where would we be today without civilisations such as the Sumerians who we are still learning from? More importantly, how did the Sumerians instantly appear, complete with so much knowledge, if they themselves were the first and had nobody from whom to copy and learn?

Found in the early 20th century in Columbia along the Magdalena river, are some very clever examples of gold figurines made using the lost-wax process. Thought to have been made by the Tolima people 1,500 years ago, out of the hundreds of 2-3 inch figurines found, some of them bare an eerie resemblence to modern aircraft. The winged figurines couldn't be explained as insects or birds, because the wings came out from underneath the body, and the body had an upright tail fin. As an experiment, some scientists built a larger scale model, adding a motor and some landing gear. The resulting model flew just like any other aircraft.

Of all the modern aircraft, the gold figurine looks most like a space shuttle because its design includes the all-important blunt nose cone. The blunt nose cone is essential to the space shuttle because it disperses air away from the fuselage to prevent overheating while it is re-entering earth's atmosphere. The blunt nose cone has been exclusively engineered in recent years by NASA scientists.

Much has been learned in recent years about civilisations such as the Sumerians, through discoveries by archaeologists of artefacts and texts in the ruins of ancient cities such as Babylon. Originally engraved in stone and found in the library archives of ancient temples, such texts were considered by the Babylonians to be sacred. They were ritually read out in public annually as part of a New Year festival. Written thousands of years before the Bible, many of these texts bear striking resemblance to well-known biblical stories. A Babylonian legend that demonstrates similarity to the first book in the Bible, the Book of Genesis, is called *Atra-Hasis* (Old Babylonian Flood Myth).

The Babylonian version begins at that time when the minor gods have to work hard for the great gods, which eventually causes a revolt. The god Enki offers to find a solution and asks the mother goddess Ninmah to create man, to "bear the yoke". The god Enlil orders that flesh from one god be mixed with clay. From this the mother goddess makes seven human couples and decrees rules to regulate procreation. Henceforth it is mankind's destiny to reproduce themselves and labour for the gods. However, after some time, humanity fills heaven and earth with noise and clamour, disturbing the peace of the gods.

Enlil seeks to put a stop to this by sending first a plague, then famine, in order to decimate the people. His plans are foiled by Enki, who instructs Atra-hasis ("the exceedingly wise") to counteract the threat with appropriate measures, such as to bring offerings, to the gods of healing and grain. Enlil is furious at the failure of his methods and decides to send a devastating flood to eradicate mankind once and for all.

He makes the gods swear an oath of allegience, but again Enki betrays his plan to Atra-hasis, appearing to him in a dream where he speaks to the reed-wall. He tells Atra-hasis to build a boat and load it with his family and various species of animals. When the flood is released, they are safe in the boat while everyone else is drowned. The gods are in great distress, especially the mother goddess, who mourns the fate of her creatures. When the flood has subsided and Atra-hasis makes his first sacrifice, Enlil is furious that he has been tricked again. However, Enki points out that the gods rely on mankind's support.

Another Babylonian legend that displays similarity to the Book of Genesis, was originally engraved in cuneiform script and is now titled *The Epic of Gilgamesh*, Tablet 11.

Utnapishtim is a citizen of the Babylonian town of Shurrupak, when he receives a message from the god Ea (through the brick wall) that the gods are about to bring a deluge. Ea instructs him to build a boat, gives him the exact measurements, and warns him to tell his inquisitive fellow-citizens that he is preparing to live with Ea in his watery abode below the Earth. When the vessel is finished, he loads it with his family, silver and gold, and all species of living creatures. At the appointed time the dams burst, the ground-waters swell and the rains come down. The storm is so fierce that even the gods "cower like dogs".

On the seventh day the flood subsides, and when Utnapishtim opens a vent to look out, he realises that the ship has run aground. He lets out a dove, which, finding no resting place, returns to the vessel. The swallow fares no better, and eventually he lets fly a raven, which eats and flies about and does not return to the boat.

Utnapishtim then disembarks with his family and makes a sacrifice, pouring out libations and burning incense. The gods smelling the sweet savour gather like flies about the priest and his offering. The mother goddess Ninmah arrives, grieving over the destruction of her creatures and vowing never to forget what has happened. She blames the god Enlil for the almost total annihilation of mankind. Although Enlil is furious that one human family has escaped, Ea soothes his anger and confesses that it was he who engineered Utnapishtim's escape. Enlil assuaged, blesses the flood-hero and his wife and grants them eternal life.

Now let's compare *Atra-Hasis* and the Gilgamesh tablet to this, its partner in the Bible, Genesis chapters 6:13, 14, 19, 7:4, 10, 20, 8:4, 6, 7, 8, 12, 20, 21.

> And God said unto Noah, The end of all flesh is come before me; for the earth is filled with violence through them; and, behold, I will destroy them with the earth.
>
> Make thee an ark of gopher wood; rooms shalt thou make in the ark, and shalt pitch it within and without with pitch.
>
> And of every living thing of all flesh, two of every sort shalt thou bring into the ark, to keep them alive with thee; they shall be male and female.
>
> For yet seven days, and I will cause it to rain upon the earth forty days and forty nights; and every living substance that I have made will I destroy from off the face of the earth.
>
> And it came to pass after seven days, that the waters of the flood were upon the earth.
>
> Fifteen cubits upward did the waters prevail; and the mountains were covered.
>
> And the ark rested in the seventh month, on the seventeenth day of the month, upon the mountains of Ararat.

> And it came to pass at the end of forty days, that Noah opened the window of the ark which he had made.
>
> And he sent forth a raven, which went forth to and fro, until the waters were dried up from off the Earth.
>
> Also he sent forth a dove from him, to see if the waters were abated from off the face of the ground.
>
> And he stayed yet other seven days; and sent forth the dove; which returned not again unto him any more.
>
> And Noah built an altar unto the Lord; and took of every clean beast, and of every clean fowl, and offered burnt offerings on the altar.
>
> And the lord smelled a sweet savour; and the Lord said in his heart, I will not again curse the ground any more for mans sake.

Many scholars believe today that the Babylonian texts form the basis for what was written in the Book of Genesis. Babylon itself is mentioned in the Bible as "Babel" in Genesis chapter 11:9.

> Therefore is the name of it called Babel; because the Lord did there confound the language of all the earth …

If we consider that the Book of Genesis had its origins in the Babylonian texts, we can find evidence of this by looking in the Bible. For example Genesis chapter 1:26.

> And God said, Let us make man in our image, after our likeness.

In this quotation the words "us" and "our" clearly denote that god is in conference with other divine entities like himself. He could not be talking to a man because man had not yet been created. This plural assignation for God seems to be at odds with the common belief that God is singular. However, when you read the equivalent Babylonian story of creation, the decision to create man was made by the council of the gods, and this is what is reflected in the Bible.

This same scene of god in conference is repeated in Genesis chapter 11:6, 7.

> And the Lord said, Behold the people is one, and they have all one language; and this they begin to do; and now nothing will be restrained from them, which they have imagined to do.
>
> Go to, let us go down, and there confound their language, that they may not understand one another's speech.

In this chapter the words "let us go down" make it clear that from his abode above the Lord is in conference with others like himself, discussing the people below.

In Genesis chapter 6:1, 2, 3, 4 God is definitely not alone.

> And it came to pass, when men began to multiply on the face of the earth, and daughters were born unto them:
>
> That the sons of God saw the daughters of men that they were fair; and they took them wives of all which they chose.
>
> And the Lord said, My spirit shall not always strive with man, for that he also is flesh: yet his days shall be an hundred and twenty years.
>
> There were giants in the earth in those days; and also after that, when the sons of God came in unto the daughters of men, and they bare children to them, the same became mighty men which were of old, men of renown.

In this verse God is said to have had many sons who gave him grandchildren. It seems reasonable to assume here that God must also have had a wife since the Bible clearly states that his sons needed wives to have children.

Another interesting situation arises in Genesis chapter 2:21, 22, 23, 24.

> And the Lord God caused a deep sleep to fall upon Adam, and he slept and he took one of his ribs, and closed up the flesh instead thereof;
>
> And the rib, which the Lord God had taken from man, made he a woman, and brought her unto the man.
>
> And Adam said, This is now bone of my bones, and flesh of my flesh; she shall be called Woman, because she was taken out of man.

> Therefore shall a man leave his father and his mother, and shall cleave unto his wife; and they shall be one flesh.

In this verse God is introducing Adam, the first man ever created, to the first woman. Why then is Adam talking about leaving his parents? The bible says Adam was the first person ever created, so he could not have had parents. This question is never answered in the Bible but it leads the reader to assume that there is more to this story than has ever been told in the Bible.

Babylon is known today as having been located in the biblical land of Eden on the river Euphrates, as one of the cities belonging to the oldest civilisation found on Earth; the Sumerians. Babylon's location in the land of the Sumerians is mentioned in the Bible. In the Book of Genesis, Sumeria is called "Shinar", Genesis chapters 10:10, 11:2.

> And the beginning of his kingdom was Babel, and Erech, and Accad, and Calneh, in the land of Shinar.

> And it came to pass, as they journeyed from the east, that they found a plain in the land of Shinar; and they dwelt there.

This quotation from the Bible mentions three cities together that are located in the land of Shinar, they are Babel, Erech, and Accad. In a map of the Ancient Near East, three cities with remarkably similar names to the ones mentioned in the Bible, are shown located together along the River Euphrates. They are Babylon, and Uruk, and Akkad, in the land of the Sumerians.

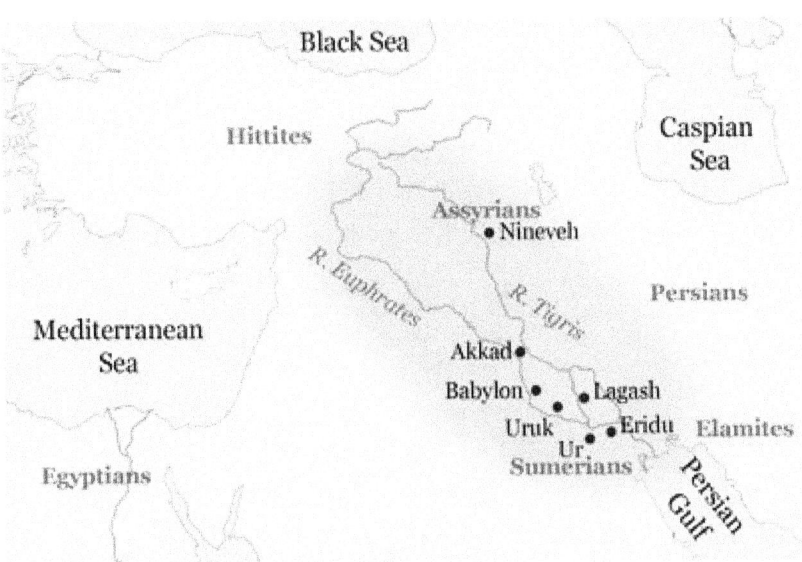

The Bible names the river Euphrates as being one of the rivers connected to the Garden of Eden in Genesis chapter 2:10, 11, 12, 14.

> And a river went out of Eden to water the garden; and from thence it was parted, and became into four heads.
>
> The name of the first is Pison: that is it which compasseth the whole land of Havilah, where there is gold;
>
> And the gold of that land is good; there is bdellium and the onyx stone.
>
> And the name of the second river is Gihon: the same is it that compasseth the whole land of Ethiopia.
>
> And the name of the third river is Hiddekel: that is it which goeth toward the east of Assyria. And the fourth river is Euphrates.

The river Euphrates was central to the Sumerians and its importance to them can be seen in an excerpt from the Babylonian creation epic called Enuma-Ellish.

> Marduk splits open the prostrate body of Tiamat whose lower part he fixes above to form the sky, complete with stars and planets. The upper part becomes the earth, and the Tigris and Euphrates flow from her eye-sockets. Her knotted tail serves as a plug to keep the waters of Apsu from flooding the land. Solid pillars separate heaven and earth. The

Tablets of Destiny he hands over to Anu for safe-keeping, and then he is officially installed by the assembled gods. Kingu, blamed for causing the revolt, is executed and from his blood and clay Ea creates man, imposing the services of the gods upon him which frees the Annunaki gods from labour. In gratitude they build a sanctuary for Marduk, which he names Babylon. Then all the gods sit down to celebrate.

In this excerpt we are told that the earth, planets and stars were created during a battle between the god Marduk and the Goddess Tiamat. The battle eventuates with Marduk being victorious, leaving the body of the goddess Tiamat in two pieces. The lower half of her body becomes the planets and stars. The upper half of Tiamat's body becomes the earth, with the rivers Tigris and Euphrates flowing from her eye-sockets. The key to fully understanding the Epic of Creation, is to realise that the gods being referred to can actually represent planets. Ancient Babylonians referred to the planets by the names of their gods, just as today all of the planets in our solar system bear the names of ancient gods.

The Book of Genesis tells us that the native land of Abram is the Sumerian city of Ur. Genesis chapter 11:28, 31.

> And Haran died before his father Terah in the land of his nativity, in Ur of the Chaldees.

> And Terah took Abram his son, and Lot the son of Haran his son's son, and Sarai his daughter in law, his son Abram's wife; and they went forth with them from Ur of the Chaldees, to go into the land of Canaan, and they came unto Haran, and dwelt there.

The location of Ur is also on the river Euphrates. The fact that the Bible tells us that Abram was from the Sumerian city of Ur, suggests that his ancestors all the way back to Adam were also citizens of the Sumerian civilisation. In effect, the Genesis section of the bible chronicles the history of the Sumerian civilisation.

The episode of Abram coming from Ur is of great importance in the Book of Genesis. It is Abram who makes a covenant with god, and from the patriarch's seed, numberless as the stars, sprang the children of Israel. Genesis chapter 15:5.

> And he brought him forth abroad, and said, Look now toward heaven, and tell the stars, if thou be able to number them; and he said unto him, So shall thy seed be.

The importance of Ur as the origin of much of today's world, is a good reason to consider some of the discoveries made by archaeologists in the ruins of the ancient city. Ur was first discovered unknowingly in 1854 by J.E. Taylor, buried under dirt mounds. Taylor found some cylinder-shaped stones engraved with a strange wedge-shaped cuneiform script. Not a lot of attention was paid to the cylinders to begin with - in fact it wasn't until after the first world war when they were first translated, that they first discovered that the stones said the ziggurat was built by a Sumerian king named Ur Nammu who reigned from 2113 to 2046 BC. The realisation that this could be the city of Ur of the Book of Genesis aroused a new interest, and in 1923 an Anglo-American expedition headed by Sir Leonard Woolley revealed the full grandeur of Ur.

Woolley uncovered temples, storehouses, workshops, spacious dwellings and countless articles used in every day Sumerian life. In a royal cemetery dating back to 4,000 BC, was discovered a wealth of treasures made in gold, silver, bronze, lapis lazuli, and other precious materials. Through the work of Woolley and his archaeologists, a picture of an astonishingly advanced people was emerging.

The urban culture that flourished on the lower Euphrates is known as Sumer and is seen as a turning point in the history of mankind.

In Ur, they discovered the people were proficient with pottery, weaving, metalwork, irrigation, dykes, reservoirs, ox-drawn ploughs, and wheeled wagons. Sailing ships were used to trade in stone, timber, and metal ores. The largest cargo vessels had capacities of up to 36 tonnes.

In the sixth year of his investigations, Woolley unearthed the royal cemetery. Dated to about 2,800 BC there were about 2,000 graves. Only a few of the graves were left intact and unlooted, but there, the excavators struck gold. In one tomb was found nine fantastic headdresses for women, shaped from lapis lazuli and carnelian, hung with gold beaten flat in the shape of beech and willow trees.

In the same tomb was a wonderful ornamental harp with an impressively realistic bull's head made from gold, with eyes of lapis lazuli.

It must be said that if the craftsmen who made the instruments were so meticulous, so too must have been the musicians who played them.

A mosaic found in Ur shows depictions of peaceful times and of war. One side shows soldiers with helmets and axes and spears.

On the other side is showing a royal feast enjoyed with music played on the lyre, while servants are bringing food.

The glimmer of gold was everywhere, untarnished after nearly 5,000 years. The exquisite artistry of the early dynasty goldsmiths does not seem to have been matched in any later period.

A golden sculpture of a ram against a flowering shrub was found in the royal cemetery. This masterpiece stands about 50 centimetres high and is fashioned from gold, lapis lazuli, silver, and mother-of-pearl. Gold leaf was applied by cold hammering. Embossing, soldering, and filigree work had all been mastered in the early third millennium BC.

More cylinder seals were found, similar to the ones first discovered by Taylor. A cylinder seal is a round cylinder usually made from a hard stone such as haematite, obsidian, steatite, amethyst, lapis lazuli or carnelian. These stones were then exquisitely engraved with written characters or scenes - the stones themselves are a form of engraved gemstone. The engraving was done in relief, the same as today's printing press uses letters in reverse. The cylinder was then rolled across a plaque of wet clay, which would then be fired and turned to stone, leaving a positive impression of a written or a pictographic text that would last indefinitely.

The benefit of using the cylinder was that texts could be mass-produced and could contain a seal of authenticity. The idea of the rolling cylinder that prints, works on the same principle as the first steam-powered rotary press that wasn't invented until the 19th century. If we have the opinion that clay stone tablets are primitive, then we should ask ourselves this question; if we were to bury together a stone cuneiform tablet, a book, and a computer, and then unearth them after 10,000 years, which one out of the three would be most likely to survive and contain retrievable information?

The residents of Ur had leather saddles and harnesses for riding, goats' hair and sheeps' wool was spun on wheels and woven into either rough or fine fabric to make bags and carpets. Young children were sent to school to learn about commerce, arithmetic and the Sumerian cuneiform script which had a 600-syllable alphabet. Fields were ploughed with wooden plough shares, fitted with funnels through which the seed was sown. This apparatus was the first known seed drill. No comparable device was used in western Europe until the Englishman Jethro Tull reinvented the seed drill in the 18th century AD. Among the fruit and vegetables that were planted were wheat, corn, pomegranates, onions, lentils, cucumbers, gourds, and melons.

The capital of Ur was almost entirely surrounded by water, extended from the Euphrates by a man-made canal. Two harbours were protected by the ramparts to the north and west, with docks, warehouses and quays. Trade in gold, incence, and lapis lazuli was conducted by land, sea, and river. The city covered an area of 60 hectares and was estimated to house 24,000 people. Towering above all other buildings was the ziggurat, a great staged pyramid dedicated to the moon god Nanna/Sin, patron deity of Ur. The ziggurat was a man-made mountain, a place where the plain-dwellers could be brought closer to their gods. At the very top of the ziggurat was the temple of the moon god Nanna/Sin. A nearby temple was dedicated to Ningal, wife of Nanna/Sin.

The moon god was known in Sumerian as Nanna and in Akkadian as Sin. Nanna was the son of the god Enlil, and Enlil's wife, the goddess Ninlil. Nanna was father of twins, Utu/Shamash the sun god and Innana/Ishtar, the goddess of the planet Venus. The Wilderness of Sin is mentioned in the Bible as being a place where the Israelites wandered during the exodus (Exodus 16:1). The word sin does not refer to sinfulness but is an untranslated word that means moon and is associated with the god Nanna/Sin. The location of the area today is not exactly known, but it is thought to be somewhere near the Sinai Peninsula and Mount Sinai, both of which have names associated with the moon god, and is where God gave Moses the ten commandments.

The biggest surprise of all was found while digging below the royal cemetery. There the archaeologist discovered a three-metre layer of silt interrupting the continuous evidence of prehistoric human inhabitation. There were broken vessels dating back to 4,000 BC, both above and below the clay. The clean clay was indeed a flood deposit; evidence of some massive inundation, Woolley believed at first that the deluge was so great as to have completely engulfed the whole valley of the Tigris and the Euphrates. Was this, then, the flood of the Book of Genesis?

Many of the questions concerning the origin of the Sumerians still remain unanswered, however, the legacy they left us of engraved texts and legends is a good place to look for clues. A Sumerian legend of Enmesh and Enten (Summer and Winter), gives us a good insight into the world in which the Sumerians lived.

In the legend, when the god Enlil conceives the idea of making the earth fertile with plants and animals, he creates two brothers, Enmesh and Enten, to bring his work to completion. Enten is in charge of the animals: causing the ewe to give birth to the lamb, the goat to the kid, cow and calf to multiply. He populates the land with wild donkeys, sheep and goats, fills the sky with birds and the rivers with fish. He plants palm-groves, fruit-trees and lays out gardens. Enmesh takes over from there by founding cities with houses and temples as high as mountains. Having accomplished these tasks the brothers come to Enlil and present him with gifts that symbolise their achievements. Enmesh brings wild and domestic animals and plants, Enten offers precious metals and stones, trees and fish. They start to quarrel as to who has more merit and ask Enlil to decide. The great god declares that Enten, who is in charge of irrigation, the basis of Sumerian agriculture, can justly call himself "farmer of the gods". The brothers acknowledge this judgement. Enmesh bends his knee to Enten, they exchange gifts and pour libations to Enlil.

Another legend, that of Lahar and Ashnan (Cattle and Grain), presents us with similar themes.

The legend goes like this: in the beginning, Anu created the Annunaki gods. However, because the world was not yet fully organised, they had to eat grass with their mouths like sheep and drink water fom a ditch. Then Lahar, the cattle goddess, and Ashnan the grain goddess, were created. They produced more food, especially milk, and things became better for the gods, but the Annunaki were still not satisfied. At this point, the god Enlil, advised by the god Enki, decides to send the goddesses to Earth. They set up sheepfolds for Lahar and present a plough and a yoke to Ashnan. In this way agriculture and animal husbandry are brought to Earth. Mankind, destined for the service of the gods, is now able to supply the gods with abundant and suitable sustenance. However, the two goddesses begin to quarrel, each denigrating the contribution of the other and praising her own advantages. Enki and Enlil intervene and Ashnan is declared the winner.

The legends of Enmesh and Enten, and of Lahar and Ashnan, reminds us of the biblical story of Cain and Abel, in Genesis chapter 4:1, 2, 3, 4, 5.

> And Adam knew Eve his wife; and she conceived, and bare Cain, and said, I have gotten a man from the Lord.
>
> And she again bare his brother Abel. And Abel was a keeper of sheep, but Cain was a tiller of the ground.
>
> And in process of time it came to pass, that Cain brought of the fruit of the ground an offering unto the Lord.
>
> And Abel, he also brought of the firstlings of his flock and of the fat thereof. And the Lord had respect unto Abel and to his offering:
>
> But unto Cain and to his offering he had not respect. And Cain was very wroth, and his countenance fell.

If you are one of the people who questions Earth's beginnings, you may have chosen to do your own research. *Genesis Unzipped* attempts to save you years of personal research by combining theories from many fields to reveal some interesting possibilities. With the Book of Genesis I will combine what is known today by modern science. Added to that are theories of ancient aliens, information provided by the Babylonian and Sumerian texts, and some never-before-published theories by the author to create one cohesive story.

There is a genuine reason for wanting to find an accurate retelling of Earth's history. That is because we like to use this information to make the most accurate prediction for Earth's future, so we can prepare ourselves for what is to come.

In the final chapter of this book we will do this and answers will be revealed when we take a close look at *Genesis Unzipped*.

Genesis Unzipped

Part 2
Contents

Part 1 5

Part 2 31

CHAPTER ONE: In the Beginning 33

CHAPTER TWO: Planet X 41

CHAPTER THREE: Creation... 49

CHAPTER FOUR: There Were Giants in the Earth 61

CHAPTER FIVE: And, Behold, I, Even I,
Do Bring a Flood of Waters Upon the Earth....................................... 67

CHAPTER SIX: Stairway to Heaven 73

CHAPTER SEVEN: The Beginning of Time.. 75

CHAPTER EIGHT: Babylon, Sodom and Gomorrah 83

CHAPTER NINE: The One God 89

CHAPTER TEN: A Universal Language.. 91

CHAPTER ELEVEN: What's in a Name? 101

CHAPTER TWELVE: Some Questions Answered by the Stars 111

Bibliography 117

CHAPTER ONE:
In the Beginning

Genesis chapter 1:1, 2, 3, 4, 5.

In the beginning God created heaven and the earth.

And the earth was without form, and void; and darkness was upon the face of the deep. And the Spirit of God moved upon the face of the waters.

And God said, Let there be Light: and there was light.

And God saw the light, that it was good; and God divided the light from the darkness.

And God called the light Day, and the darkness he called Night.

And the evening and the morning were the first day.

Our story begins with the sun, which is eternal.

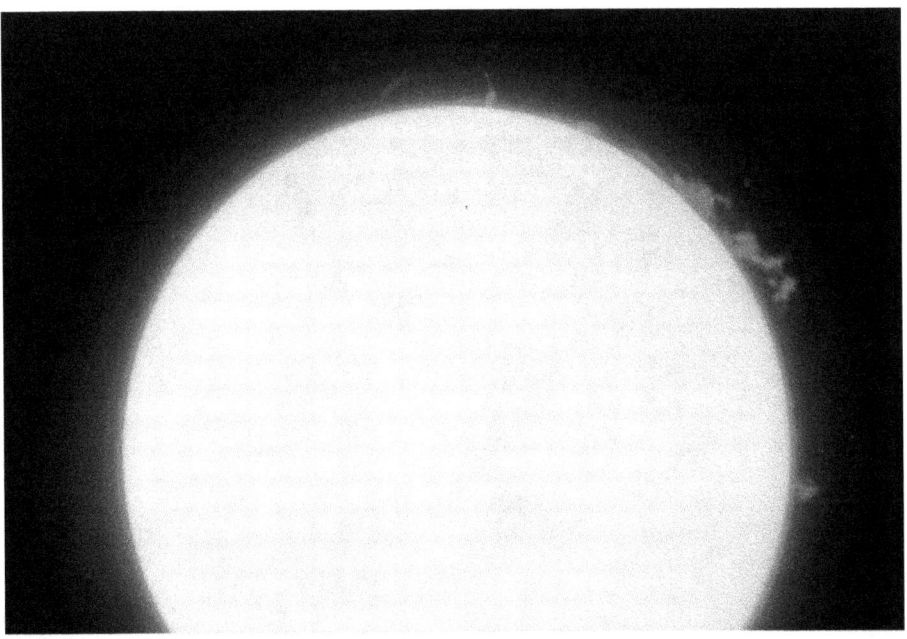

Billions of years ago the surface of the sun evolved a volcano, so hot and huge that periodically it erupted large amounts of matter into space that slowly cooled and formed into the planets of our solar system. We know because of the many active volcanoes on our own planet that the interior of the earth is molten. The crust of the earth is not molten, indicating to us that the earth is still in the process of cooling. Because the earth is in the process of cooling now, we know that the earth originally at one time was completely molten, like its progenitor the sun.

The planets of our solar system all share a common orbit on the ecliptic plane because of their relationship to the common origin. The ecliptic plane would line up with the same position of the Sun that gave birth to all the planets of our solar system. From the inner to the outer solar system they are: the sun, Mercury, Venus, Mars, Earth and its satellite moon, Jupiter, Saturn and its satellite Pluto, Uranus and Neptune - a family of planets.

The increased magnetic field of our solar system created by the new planets attracted a planet from a nearby star system. The invading planet from another system had a retrograde orbit to Earth. It was orbiting at an incline to the ecliptic and was set to cross the ecliptic plane between Jupiter and Mars. At this time, Earth had no life. Earth was one solid landmass, completely engulfed in one large body of water. Earth also orbited the ecliptic plane between Jupiter and Mars and, however unlikely but not impossible, the two planets were on a collision course.

The ensuing collision of planets eventuated with the watery Earth being broken in half by the invading planet.

Genesis chapter 1:6, 7:

And God said, Let there be a firmament in the midst of the waters, and let it divide the waters from the waters.

And God made the firmament, and divided the waters which were under the firmament from the waters which were above the firmament: and it was so.

One half of Earth crumbled into watery asteroids and continued to orbit between Mars and Jupiter in what is today known as the asteroid belt.

Genesis chapter 1:8:

And God called the firmament Heaven. And the evening and the morning were the second day.

The other half of Earth with its moon still orbiting was thrust into a new orbit between Venus and Mars.

The moon had been inundated by a meteor storm caused by a collision of planets. The moon, once an unblemished pearl in the sky, was now left scarred and full of craters.

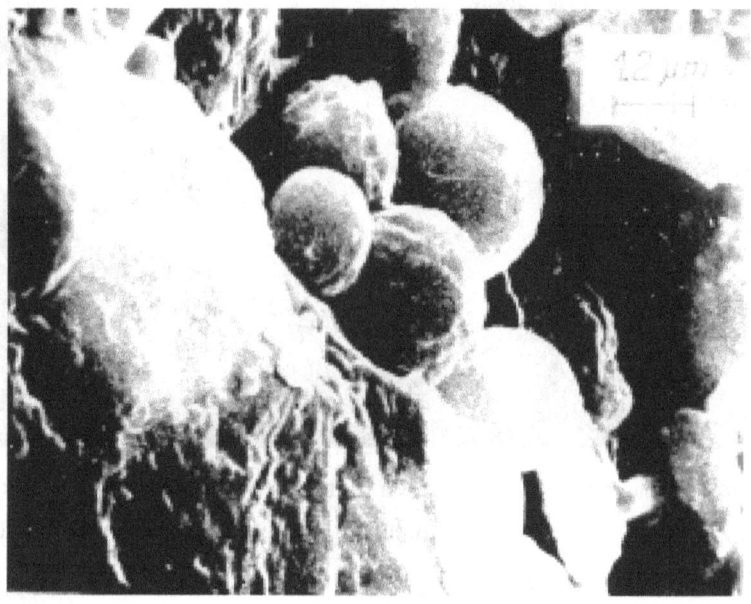

Parts of the invading planet with living matter also landed on the moon. These died however because the moon was incapable of sustaining life. Moon rocks found in recent times show fossilised remains of tiny living organisms, with no explanation as to how they suddenly appeared and then died.

Other parts of the invading planet with water crumbled and fell into their own orbits and became the comets. The comets' orbits traced, to varying degrees, the orbit of the invading planet. The orbits were retrograde, elliptical, at an incline to the ecliptic and went for many years. The closest point to Earth that their orbits returned them to was the asteroid belt.

Just as the orbit of Halley's comet returns it to the point of collision, the asteroid belt, so too did the orbit of the invading planet. It now has a destiny to maintain that orbit forever. An orbit so long that it now circles two star systems. In the time the invading planet completes one orbit, the Earth will have completed 3,600 orbits.

The earth continued to stabilise after the collision. What was left was like a hemisphere topped with water. As this was revolving in space the gravitational tendency was to return the remains of the planet back to a spherical shape. The first thing to happen was that the water rushed into the space where there was half a planet missing, then dry land appeared for the first time.

> Genesis chapter 1:9:
>
> And God said, let the waters under the heaven be gathered together unto one place, and let the dry land appear: and it was so.

Nowadays we can look at a globe of the Earth and see that approximately half of the Earth is water, with most of the water being concentrated in the southern hemisphere.

> Genesis chapter 1:10:
>
> And God called the dry land Earth; and the gathering together of the waters called he the Seas: and God saw that it was good.

The remaining hemisphere-shaped piece of Earth started to crack into the familiar-shaped continents we know today, while the land and the water became balanced. The water rushed into the cracks, forcing the continents further apart until eventually a balance was reached. This is today what we call continental drift.

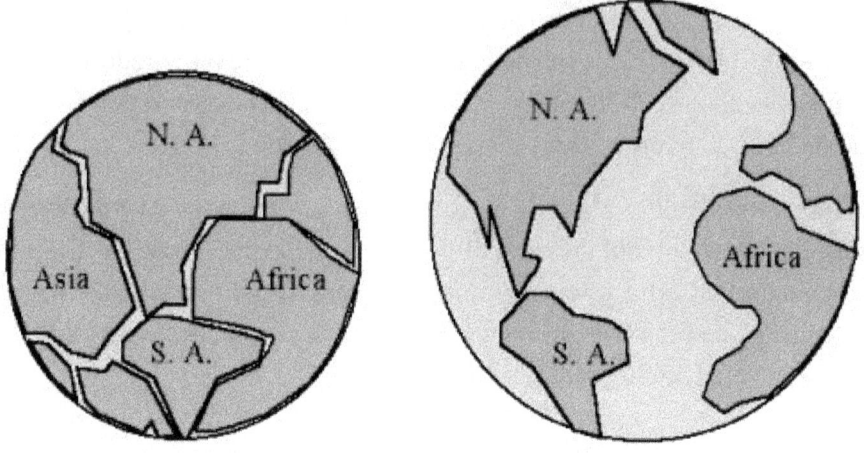

The cracks between continents ran so deep that they reached the centre of Earth. This caused volcanic eruptions under the oceans which hardened and became the underwater mountain ranges known as the mid-Atlantic and mid-Pacific ridges.

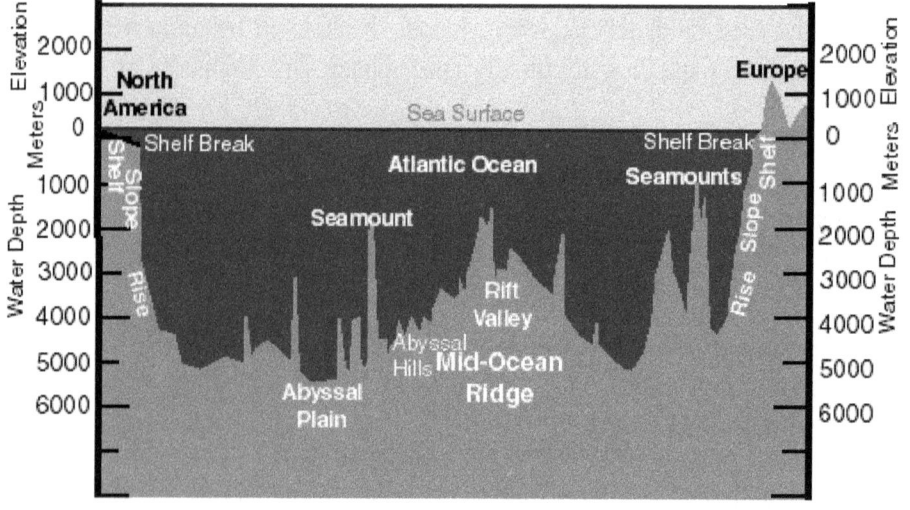

The Earth was now cracked and shaken and had many tectonic plates and fault lines. The thickness of Earth's crust was now inconsistent. However, parts of the invading planet that contained the seed of life also fell to Earth. Earth was now capable of sustaining life, and so began life on Earth, a planet that was at least a billion years old.

Genesis chapter 1:11, 12.

And God said, Let the Earth bring forth grass, the herb yielding seed, and the fruit tree yielding fruit after his kind, whose seed is in itself, upon the earth; and it was so.

And the earth brought forth grass, and herb yielding seed after his kind, and the tree yielding fruit, whose seed was in itself, after his kind; and God saw that it was good.

CHAPTER TWO:
Planet X

Now a permanent member of our solar system, the invading planet has become Planet Number Ten, or in Roman numerals, X. For this reason and because it is the planet that crosses our solar system, we will call it Planet X.

The grand orbit of Planet X takes it deep into space away from both suns, and brings it back close to the sun when it crosses our solar system once every 3,600 years. It survives this orbit because the planet is very volcanic, giving it a thick atmosphere. This causes a greenhouse effect, in which it retains heat during its journey far into space and then shields the planet from excess sunlight when it crosses our solar system.

At the time of the collision when Earth was barren, life had already existed on Planet X for millions of years. Astronomers on Planet X kept records of events by engraving clay tablets and keeping them logged in a sacred library. Clay and stone were chosen for their durability for the reason that this would make them available for generations, years into the future. Evolution on Planet X had started millions of years ahead of Earth. On Planet X people were very intelligent and civilised, highly spiritual and very much connected with their higher power, at a time when there was no intelligent life on Earth.

Because of the lengthy orbit of the planet, the inhabitants evolved lengthy life spans. If an average life span for a person of Earth was 70 orbits, an average life span of 70 orbits on Planet X would make them 70 x 3,600 Earth years. If a person with such a long life span were to live on Earth among humans, they would be seen by the humans as godlike and having an eternal life.

In time, after many orbits, Planet X slowly cooled and lost some of its greenhouse gases, exposing the planet to extremes of heat and cold. The leaders of the planet declared this an environmental disaster and so tried to increase volcanic activity by exploding awesome weapons in the craters of the volcanos.

When this failed, a new plan was launched to restore the greenhouse effect that was essential to life on Planet X. The new idea was to heat gold to extremely high temperatures and transmute it to a monatomic state. The powder created was so fine that one particle equaled one atom of gold. This fine powder was then spread above the atmosphere, producing the life-saving greenhouse effect. The powder that was so fine was lighter than the atmosphere and so did not return easily to the surface of the planet. Instead it protected the planet with a shield made from gold.

On Earth today there is a name for the gold transmuted to powder, sought by alchemists for many centuries: it is called the Philosopher's Stone.

Although technically this was a solution, a large amount of gold was needed for this idea to succeed. On Planet X gold was very scarce and so the gold needed to be found on another planet. The scriptures that were engraved many orbits earlier, told of a time when Planet X collided with Earth, breaking Earth into two pieces, the wound exposing the golden veins of the planet. Many believed the collision story was only mythology. However, no better alternatives were found so the search started, to find the gold of Earth. The richest veins of gold would be located at the heart of the planet. The land that resembled the heart of Earth became the destination for the first Earth landing.

The first intelligent life on Earth arrived many thousands of years ago. After travelling through space by celestial craft from Planet X, 600 inhabitants formed the first Earth colony. Civilisation existed on three levels.

200 occupied Upper Earth. Their task was to live in space as watchers of Earth. They would maintain the celestial craft in space and deliver gold, supplies, people, and messages between Earth and Planet X.

200 occupied Middle Earth. Their task was the administration of the colony. They would live on the surface of the Earth in the region between the rivers Tigris and the Euphrates. We now know this area today as ancient Mesopotamia. Here would meet the council of 12 that included members of the royal family. They were known to the colony by their positions as the greater gods. The gods were involved in making decisions and management of the colony.

Two hundred occupied Lower Earth. Their task was to mine the gold that was so badly needed by their home planet. They would occupy the area below the surface of the Earth where the gold was located, underground. Among the inhabitants of Earth, these were the rank & file, the minor gods, charged with the most laborious of all the tasks.

Today we divide our planet into latitude and longitude so we can pinpoint certain areas of the globe. At that time the planet Earth was attributed human characteristics to label the planet in a certain way for ease of navigation. For example, the administrative centre in Mesopotamia was known as the Navel of the Earth. Imagine the planet was a person standing; the head would be the northern hemisphere. The person's underside was the southern hemisphere. For this reason, the land of the south was also called the Underworld. The gold was mined in the Underworld in the area we call today South Africa. Similar to the Underworld, because of its southerly location, Australia has today earned the name "The Land Down Under".

From Lower Earth in the Underworld, the gold was transported to Middle Earth, the navel of the Earth in Mesopotamia. Here they had facilities to launch the gold through Upper Earth, forward to Planet X. The distance to Planet X varied greatly. For most of its orbit it was completely inaccessible because it was so far away. It was only reachable for a short time when its orbit returned it closest to Earth at the original point of collision, the asteroid belt. This too posed difficulties, to ship large quantities of gold long distances in a small timeframe. Large craft with enormous amounts of fuel would be required to overcome the gravitational pull of Earth if shipping the gold direct, however there was an easier way. Gold would be shipped by shuttlecraft in regular amounts and stored on Mars awaiting the return of Planet X. The storage process would be completed while Planet X was far away in space. When Planet X returned to the asteroid belt, all the gold could then be shipped in one large load direct from Mars. The trip from Mars was much closer than from Earth and less fuel was needed to launch the large craft because Mars had a much weaker gravitational pull than Earth. This required the establishment of a base on Mars for the purpose of gold storage and forwarding on to Planet X.

Eventually, after much planning and preparation, the plan was a success and gold started to flow on to Planet X, ensuring the future and safety of the planet. To show Earth their appreciation and in exchange for the gold that was removed, Earth was given the gift of domestic plants and animals from Planet X. It was important for the colonists to eat the sort of food that was familiar to them as they did on their home planet.

Many of the local plants and animals were distasteful. For this reason a House of Creation was established in the land known as ancient Mesopotamia, located between the rivers Tigris and Euphrates. The purpose was to adapt the domestic flora and fauna from Planet X to thrive on Earth. Some of the gifts from Planet X to Earth were: cattle, pigs, sheep, goats, chickens, horses, donkeys, palm-groves, wheat, barley, rye, spelt, beans, peas, lentils, olives, apples, figs, grapes, hops, lotus, roses, pistachios, and many more. The introduction of plants and animals from their home planet would make life on Earth much more like living on Planet X. Earth would be a much more hospitable and civilised place. It is for this reason that ancient Mesopotamia is known today as "the cradle of civilisation" and "the fertile crescent".

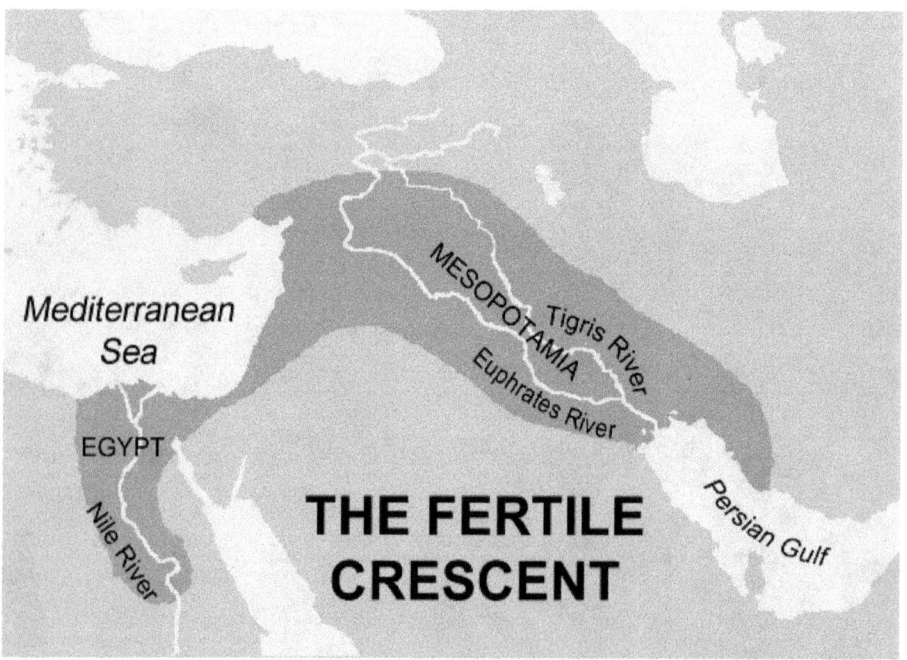

The area known as the fertile crescent and what was once known as Middle Earth are one and the same. The largest sea to border onto this land is called the Mediterranean. Translated into English, the word Mediterranean means Middle Earth. Therefore, the Mediterranean Sea is literally the sea of Middle Earth.

The House of Creation was a critical part of Earth colony. It was not only valued for its assistance in providing food but its association with herbs and medicine made it a centre for healing colonists who were sick or had accidents. To establish its uniqueness and define its purpose, the symbol chosen for their logo was of entwined serpents. Today the symbol for medical associations around the world is still the same.

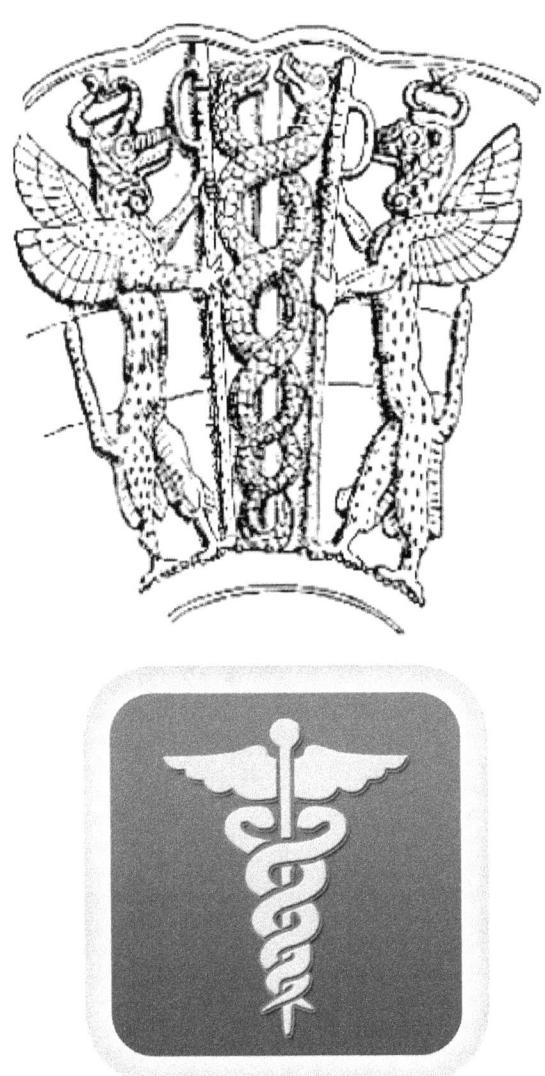

CHAPTER THREE:
Creation

Success for the colony on Earth lasted for many orbits of Planet X. For the colonists living on Earth it seemed an eternity. The task was particularly laborious for the inhabitants of Lower Earth. The work for them was relentless. Here the inhabitants had spent thousands of years underground doing backbreaking work digging for gold, where it was dark and hot. The small amount of light came from fires that only made it hotter and full of smoke. There came a time when they started to ask themselves, was it worth saving their home planet if they were never going to see it? They could make a better life for themselves on Earth no matter what happened to their home planet. To this end, the inhabitants of Lower Earth decided to put down their tools in disagreement with the greater gods. No longer would they mine gold for Planet X.

The ancient word for opposition was Satan. The sudden rebellion of Lower Earth was the first appearance of Satan in that it was the first opposition to the mining plans of Earth's colony. A meeting of the council of the gods was called to discuss how to restore gold production in Lower Earth and how to overcome their opposition, Satan.

In the Council of the Gods, much discussion was taking place. It was clear that what was needed was workers to mine the gold in the Underworld. The Lord of the House of Creation suggested that the gods create the workmen required, by upgrading an existing species from Earth, and give it characteristics of the gods from Planet X. That way they could let them do all the fishing, tending to the fowl and the cattle, and they could even protect the gods against the many creepy things that roam the earth.

Genesis chapter 1:26:

And God said, Let us make man in our image, after our likeness: and let them have dominion over the fish of the sea, and over the fowl of the air, and over the cattle, and over all the earth, and over every creeping thing that creepeth upon the earth.

In this way, the greater gods and the minor gods could live in leisure. The argument against this was that by excessively tampering with creation, they would offend the Creator of All. The new race could bring problems for which they would not be prepared. The answer to these objections was that if the Creator of All was not happy he would not allow them the capability of creating, and unless something was done to find a replacement workforce for Lower Earth, the mission on Earth would be finished.

After much discussion, the decision of the council was announced. For the purpose of doing work for the gods and relieving the gods of their workload, a new species called Humans would be created by genetically mixing the image and the likeness of the gods with a being that already existed on the Earth. The creature deemed suitable was observed on its hands and knees eating grass with its mouth and drinking water from a ditch with the rest of the wild animals. Today we refer to them as our ancestor homo erectus.

The future of Earth's colony was now dependent on the skill of the Lord of Creation. To create the new human species, DNA from a male of

Planet X was mixed in a clay test tube beaker, with a female ovary of homo erectus from Earth. The embryo created was then implanted into the womb of a mother goddess. When preparing the DNA they were able to isolate and activate only the qualities that were required for the task at hand while the rest would remain as junk DNA.

The genetic manipulation between the species from two different planets was possible because all life on Earth came from Planet X and the DNA was the same. It was the history of the genetic manipulation between the two species that gave the name to the first book of the Bible: Genesis, the book of genes.

For the first stage of creation, fourteen mother goddesses were chosen to give birth to seven male and seven female earth children, who had the image of the gods from Planet X.

Genesis chapters 1:27, 28, 5:2:

So God created man in his own image, in the image of God created he him; male and female created he them.

And God blessed them, and God said unto them, Be fruitful and multiply, and replenish the earth.

Male and female created he them; and blessed them, and called their name Adam, in the day when they were created.

In the Sumerian legends, the mother goddess who gave birth to the first male child was named Ninmah. Affectionately she was also known as Mamma or Mami. Today she is daily remembered as the mother of the human race by the constant use of her name in our language, with words such as ma, mamma, mummy and mum.

A thousands-of-years-old Sumerian wall engraving depicts Ninmah the mother goddess in the laboratory house of creation, surrounded by test tubes, beakers and tripod. She is seated with Adam on her knee. The feature in this pictograph which identifies the goddess is the horned headdress. The horned headdress is a symbol for the gods of that time the same as today a crown is the symbol for a king or queen. The latin word for horn is cornu, as is seen in the word cornucopia, meaning "horn of plenty", or the word unicorn, meaning "one horn". From the word cornu are derived the words coronial, coronary, coronation, crown, etc.

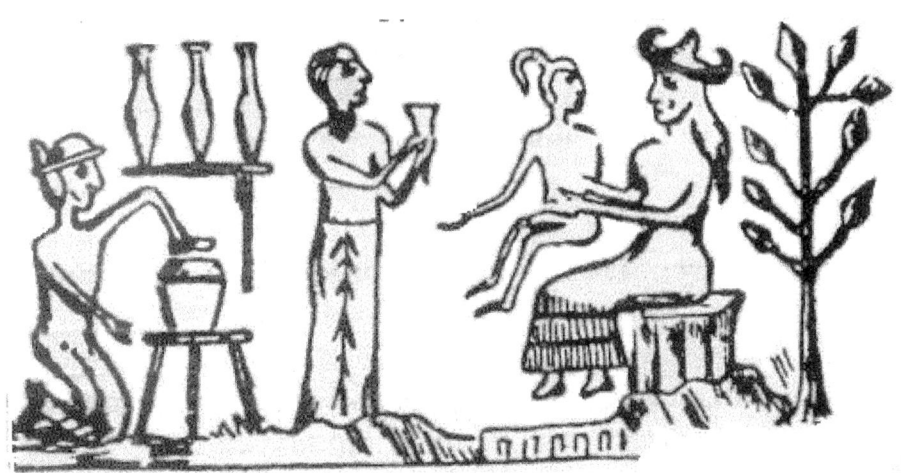

Another Sumerian engraving shows the mother goddess Ninmah and the Lord of Creation, known by his Sumerian name as Enki. The omega-shaped symbol they are holding depicts the umbilical cord, which is being held over a baby's crib and represents birth. In their hands they are holding test tube beakers. Their identity as gods is indicated above their heads by the winged globe symbol for Planet X.

All of the mother goddesses gave birth to beautiful children, however when the children had grown old enough, they were not compatible. None of the human couples were able to give birth to their own children. This failed to solve the problem because, if the race of humans could not reproduce themselves, then giving birth to more humans would only be at the expense of the mother goddesses, who suffered the pains of giving birth. This would only create more labour for the gods. Among the gods there were many who were sceptical, saying that this was proof that the Creator of All was not happy, and had forbidden to the humans the fruit of the tree of knowledge.

In Jewish folklore, as documented in the 13th century writing by Rabbi Isaac ben Jacob ha-Cohen, we are told that the first male born was named Adam. Created at the same time as Adam was his partner, a woman named Lilith.

Adam and Lilith both saw themselves as being superior to each other, and as a result, they argued over who would go on top during sex. Because of the disagreement, their union was never consummated. Lilith left the Garden of Eden to have sex with Archangel Samael, and Adam was left all alone.

Genesis chapter 2:18.

And the Lord God said, it is not good that man should be alone; I will make him an help meet for him.

To keep Adam from being alone, a partner for him needed to be created who would be more compatible. To overcome the problem of incompatibility, from the rib of Adam the first male born, was extracted a small amount of DNA. Mixed in a clay beaker, using the DNA from Adam's rib was conceived a female embryo. Today this procedure is called cloning. The baby born was known as Eve. Born to be a partner for the man, when she was old enough, she was so genetically close she was bone of his bone and flesh of his flesh.

Symbolically, Eve was created from the rib of man because the rib was neither in the front of man, or behind. The rib was on man's side. This meant that neither man or woman was given dominant position over the other. Eve's partnership with Adam was equal, and that's what she was cut out for.

In the land of Eden in an enclosed garden, laden with all the fabulous fruits and flowers from Planet X, the couple were kept in a sanctuary to be able to find each other in natural surrounds. The Lord of Creation eagerly awaited the result.

Why this couple were so special is because they were able to partake of the fruit of the tree of knowledge that had previously been forbidden to creations of the human race. In the Book of Genesis, the term knowledge, knowing, know, or knew, refers to the union between a man and a woman, specifically for the purpose of bearing children. Examples of this are given in Genesis chapter 4:1, 17, 25.

> And Adam knew Eve his wife; and she conceived, and bare Cain, and said, I have gotten a man from the Lord.

> And Cain knew his wife; and she conceived, and bare Enoch: and he builded a city, after the name of his son, Enoch.

> And Adam knew his wife again; and she bare a son, and called his name Seth: For God, said she, hath appointed me another seed instead of Abel, whom Cain slew.

The tree of knowledge is the family tree, which grows as a result of a man and a woman knowing each other.

The forbidden fruit of the tree of knowledge, is the children that were forbidden to human couples who were incompatible and could not know each other. Some examples of the use of fruit terminology to mean children or offspring, are shown in the Bible when God is creating in Genesis chapter 1:22.

> And God blessed them, saying, Be fruitful and multiply, and fill the waters in the seas, and let fowl multiply in the earth.

> God also talks to the first men and women in Genesis chapter 1:28.

> And God blessed them, and God said unto them, Be fruitful and multiply, and replenish the earth ...

> And God spoke to Noah in Genesis chapters 8:17, 9:1.

> And god blessed Noah and his sons, and said unto them, Be fruitful, and multiply, and replenish the earth.

When Adam and Eve partook of the forbidden fruit of the tree of knowledge, this meant that they were the first couple to have a loving union and bare children. With the help of the serpent of creation, the human race was born.

Now, humans could suffer their own pains when giving birth. From now on humans could look after the animals, plough the fields and do all the work, so the gods could live in leisure.

In the council of the gods, the terms of the agreement to allow the production of the human race was still being debated. Among the gods there were some who did not approve of the human race taking care of their own reproduction. They feared that in time, the gods could not control the growth in population, and that this would mean that the human race would grow into a force which would rival the gods themselves.

Genesis chapter 3:22.

And the Lord God said, Behold the man is become as one of us.

CHAPTER FOUR:
There Were Giants in the Earth

Humans were bred in exactly the same manner as any of the other domestic animals. The gods were their shepherds. In time the human species multiplied and was able to mine the gold in place of the minor gods. In fact, because their race started to multiply so rapidly the gold production was soon higher than it had ever been. The news of the new species that helped increase the gold production arrived on Planet X and was greeted with much celebration. This was seen as the Creator of All showing his kindness to Planet X. On such a momentous occasion to pay his respects to the brave crew who had defied all opposition and succeeded beyond expectations, the king of all the gods from Planet X announced he would be making a journey to Earth.

Earth began preparing for the coming of the king of Planet X. A city with monumental temples, and a mountainous ziggurat step pyramid, was built in his honour. The festivities would include every god and human from all three levels of Earth to be assembled as one in the presence of their king.

For the inhabitants of Upper Earth this was a momentous event. Very few of them had been privileged enough to visit the wondrous civilisation that had been built on Middle Earth. If they did visit quickly they would report back to people hungry for news of the wonderful life on Earth. Their position as watchers of planet Earth and pilots of the shuttlecraft between Earth and Planet X would require them to spend years away from their family, in space or on the surface of the inhospitable Mars. Among all the interest in coming to Earth, the most highly anticipated event was the meeting with the new race of humans. On the momentous day of the celebration all 200 watchers came down to Earth to be in the presence of their king. As pilots of the celestial craft they had all earned their wings, and on that day wings were worn with pride.

The 200 watchers of Earth were all male. As a requirement for their job they were all unmarried. Because none of them had reached the status of father, they were still referred to as the sons of gods. On the momentous day in the presence of their king when all wore their wings, the sons of gods saw the daughters of men were fair and they took them as wives.

Genesis chapter 6:1, 2.

And it came to pass, when men began to multiply on the face of the earth, and daughters were born unto them,

That the sons of God saw the daughters of men that they were fair; and they took them wives of all which they chose.

This mutiny of the watchers from Upper Earth was another direct opposition to the central plan and so existed as the second emergence of Satan.

Although you could hardly blame the sons of gods for their natural desire to start their own family, this caused another problem for the Earth colony.

Genesis chapter 6:3.

And the lord said, My spirit shall not always strive with man, for that he also is flesh.

Pilots were needed by the Earth colony to deliver gold and return supplies from Planet X. How could they replace the valuable two hundred watchers of Upper Earth? Another assembly was called for the council of the gods.

In finding a solution to any problem it was not unusual for the gods to look at the stars. The stars were observed and a record was kept of specific events alongside the position of the stars at that time. This was, they believed, the secret to telling the future by the stars. History was seen to be cyclical so the similar alignment of the stars was seen to correlate to similar events in history. 'What goes around comes around' was seen as fate. It was helpful to keep historical records so they could prepare for their future or solve the problems of the present by using the same solution as the past. The concept of people from Earth looking to the stars for guidance, is reflected today in the words of a popular ancient prayer, "On earth as it is in heaven".

The last time a similar situation arose it was solved by the creation of humans. To replace the watchers of Upper Earth another new breed of worker would have to be created. With the creation of humans it was shown to be possible to isolate only the desired qualities in the DNA so that an ideal worker could be made. What was required here was a creature with a small body so it would be lightweight and require minimal sustenance when in space. It would need a large head and brain for the intelligence required to pilot spacecrafts. It was most important that this creature did not wish to cohabit with humans, as did the watchers. For this reason it was created grey-coloured and lacking in human emotion so that if ever the two species met they would see each other as alien.

It was intended when creating this being that it lived out its existence not on Earth but in space and on the surface of Mars.

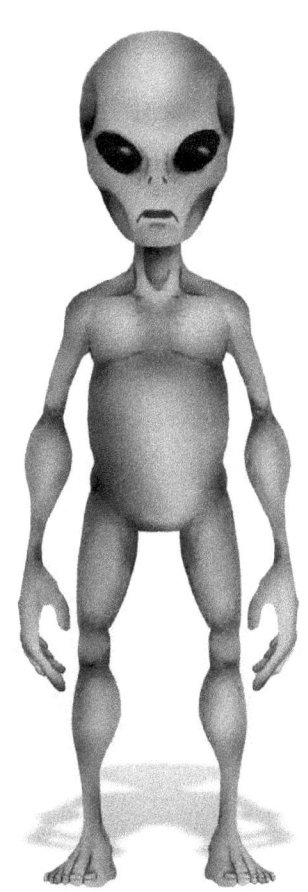

Creating a new breed of space men to pilot the shuttlecraft was another huge success. It was a fine-tuning of the operation so that soon gold began to flow on to Planet X in record quantities. The watchers that descended to Earth, the sons of gods that took the daughters of men as wives, soon had children with them. These children were cherubic and the most beautiful that had ever been born on Earth.

Genesis chapter 6:4.

There were giants in the earth in those days; and also after that, when the sons of God came in unto the daughters of men, and they bare children to them, the same became mighty men which were of old, men of renown.

A new civilisation had been born, an offspring of its parent the Earth colony. Populated by gods, demigods and humans, it was the most advanced civilisation that had ever existed, the time of Atlantis.

CHAPTER FIVE:
And, Behold, I, Even I, Do Bring a Flood of Waters Upon the Earth

Upper Earth's colony and the space-related side of the mission was now again fully operational. It was the duty of the watchers to observe Earth for any peculiar weather or anything that could affect the inhabitants on Earth. Weather on Earth could change due to the magnetic field of a nearby celestial body venturing too close to Earth. The approach of Planet X would normally cause every type of extreme weather on Earth.

At this time Earth was experiencing an ice age, but with the periodical approach of Planet X weather patterns were changing rapidly. What was evident from space was that the ice cap that was covering South Pole was starting to crumble and slide into the Pacific Ocean. This gigantic slab of ice the size of Antarctica would then melt and cause enough tidal waves and flooding to cover the whole Earth and put an end to all life.

From the first arrival of the travellers from Planet X to the imminent destruction of Earth by the coming flood, the Earth would have orbited the sun 432,000 times. With every 3,600 years on Earth equalling 1 year on Planet X, that meant that in orbits of Planet X around the sun it was 120 years.

Genesis chapter 6:3.

Yet his days shall be an hundred and twenty years.

To discuss the future of Earth's colony and the impending flood another meeting was called for the council of the gods.

Since the flood would cover the whole planet there was nowhere on Earth to escape except in orbit until the flood started to recede. The shuttlecraft normally used for carrying gold was the only means at their disposal, and limited space was available. 432,000 Earth years was a long time for the colony to grow and accumulate wealth. They would have to draw a line between who would be saved and who would remain.

The decision was reached: to let no man be told of the impending flood. This meant that only the gods who were born on Planet X and their descendants, if the spouse also was born on Planet X, would be warned and saved with the shuttlecraft. If a native of Planet X was married to a human spouse then he or she must decide whether to leave the spouse behind, or stay on Earth with the spouse and perish. Since there was nothing that could be done to save the citizens of the Earth colony and Atlantis they would not be warned of the coming deluge. The gods decided that since the flood was a natural event then it must be the will of the Creator of All to destroy all life on Earth. The gods would have no right to intervene.

To leave Earth was not a pleasant decision for the gods to make; all had sacrificed much for the sake of Earth's colony. So much knowledge and history that had been amassed over thousands of years would be lost forever. Of all the gods the Lord of Creation in particular was dismayed. All of the plants and animals and humans he had created would also be lost forever. He had sworn an oath in the council of the gods that no man would be warned of the coming deluge. He could do nothing to save them.

That night the Lord of Creation had a dream: he dreamt he was instructed by the Creator of All to build a large boat and enclose inside the seed of life so that life on Earth could survive the flood. The instructions for building the boat were handed to him engraved on a plaque of lapis lazuli. When he woke in the morning, the engraved plaque had materialised as solid and was leaning against his wall. The Creator of All had made his dream come true.

The Lord of Creation was confronted with a dilemma. He could not build the boat himself because that would be too conspicuous, and he had sworn an oath not to tell any human. Yet, his desire to obey the Creator of All was overwhelming. The Lord of Creation decided that his oath to tell no man of the coming deluge would not prevent him from giving that warning to a man's house. He needed to disguise himself so that he would go unnoticed while he was delivering the message, and not appear to be breaking his oath.

The Lord solved the problem this way. First, to disguise himself he removed all of the regalia that was befitting of a god to wear. Next, he shaved his long beard and cut his long hair. All he wore was a loincloth. A god would not normally be seen in this fashion. He then proceeded to the quarters of his faithful servant who was located inside the city. When the god reached the servant's hut he called to the man not to look upon his lord but to stay inside where he was until the god had finished his business with the wall of the reed hut. In a voice as loud as thunder, to the wall of the hut the god gave the warning of the coming deluge and gave the instructions to build a boat large enough to save the seed of life on Earth. To the wall, again he gave the warning, the number of days and nights of flooding rain would be 40. He then leant the plaque with instructions against the wall and left. He had told no man of the coming deluge.

It was not really possible for the god to know the exact number of days the rains would last. The number 40 was the number that stood for the rank of the Lord of Creation in the council of the gods. By encoding the number 40 in the message, the god was stamping it with the seal of authority by which his servant would abide. Inside the hut, the servant heard the voice of his god, like he could hear the sound of rolling thunder.

Under instructions given by his god, the servant built a boat big enough to save the seed of life, from a flood that was likely to destroy all life on Earth.

The boat was filled with people and domestic animals and grains. Only the animals created by the Earth colony, such as pigs, goats, sheep, and cattle needed to enter. Aside from the stud male stock, the female animals were all expecting offspring when they boarded the boat.

The boat was sealed with pitch throughout because the first part of the flood saw the boat completely submerged underwater. After a while when the rain settled, the boat floated to the surface.

Genesis chapter 7:17, 18, 19.

And the flood was 40 days upon the earth; and the waters increased, and bare up the ark, and it was lift up above the earth.

And the waters prevailed, and were increased greatly upon the earth; and the ark went upon the face of the waters.

And the waters prevailed exceedingly upon the earth; and all the high hills, that were under the whole heaven, were covered.

When the boat began to float on the surface, it became possible to open a doorway to the top deck. Sails were then raised so the boat could be steered to the highest land, the first to appear after the rain. With the help of a golden compass the boat reached its destination: Mt Ararat.

CHAPTER SIX:
Stairway to Heaven

Finally the occupants were able to disembark. They were hungry and decided to light a fire and cook some of the animals they had brought along for food. The gods had spent the time of the deluge observing the calamity from space. They too were hungry and landed their craft on the first hard ground to appear.

When the gods disembarked they were astonished to find humans had been able to survive the flood. In their defence, the Lord of Creation spoke up, saying that if ever the gods were to attempt to rebuild the Earth colony, they could not possibly achieve this without the help of the humans. The gods were tired of bickering - they had spent much time in space crying over what had been lost. The smell of the roasting meat pleased the gods and softened their hearts and they realised the sense in what was being said. With this concession the gods blessed the humans and bid them go forth and multiply.

> Genesis chapters 8:20, 21, 9:1.
>
> And Noah builded an altar unto the Lord; and took of every clean beast, and of every clean fowl, and offered burnt offerings on the altar.
>
> And the Lord smelled a sweet savour, and the Lord said in his heart, I will not again curse the ground for man's sake.
>
> And god blessed Noah and his sons, and said unto them, Be fruitful, and multiply, and replenish the earth.

The job of rebuilding the Earth colony was a lot of work. The cities were rebuilt by people under the instruction of their gods. Cities were built anew in exactly the same position as the olden cities, according to the original plan of Earth's colony.

The most notable feature of an ancient city was called the Temple Ziggurat, or step pyramid. This was a high rise building that rose in seven stages to the highest point above the city. On the highest level of the pyramid was located the holy temple, which was the official abode of the gods and the meeting place for the council of twelve. The temple on the top level of the pyramid represented Planet X. The very lowest level, the ground on which the pyramid was built was the Earth. The six stages of the pyramid in between the top level and the ground represented the six celestial bodies between Earth and Planet X. These are Mars, Jupiter, Saturn, Uranus, Neptune, and Pluto. All together, the seven steps that led to the gods was known as the Stairway to Heaven.

CHAPTER SEVEN:
The Beginning of Time

The people soon outnumbered the gods and so for the sake of organisation a new intermediary position was created. Kingship and priesthood was granted to the Earth as a gift from the gods. The social hierarchy was created as a means for organising and educating people. The most important components that make up a civilised society are mirrored today in ancient games such as tarot and chess.

Education was given to people in many fields: astronomy, law, maths, science, metallurgy, pottery, spinning, music, commerce, building, cooking, farming, reading, writing, engraving, and so on. Simple writing scripts were invented for humans to use in preference over the more complicated cuneiform script of the gods. Papyrus and parchment were developed for writing because they were simpler to produce than the clay tablets. Papyrus would not last for tens of thousands of years like clay but neither did humans have a long life span compared to their gods.

The calender was given to Earth as a gift from Planet X by Anu, the Sky God of the Sumerians. Today his name is echoed daily through our language. For example, an event that takes place once a year is said to be annual - the word annual derives from the name Anu. When we say this is the year 2014 AD, AD stands for the words Anno Domini, which mean year of our Lord. The word Anno, which means year, derives from the name Anu. An annulus is a circle with no beginning and no end like the constant orbit of Earth, of which one cycle equals one year. The word annulus derives from the name Anu. The occasion of the gift of time by the god Anu gave rise to the folklore legend of Father Time.

By Father Time a new system of time-keeping was created based on the movements of planet Earth. One day equals one rotation of Earth, one hour equals one twelfth of either AM or PM of one day. One year equals one orbit of the Earth around the Sun, one month equals one twelfth of one year. One aeon equals one circle of precession of the Earth's axis, one zodiac age equals one twelfth of one aeon.

The circle of the zodiacs as a method of time-keeping was very important to the council of the gods of that time. One zodiac age being equal to 2,160 orbits of the Earth was a useful intermediary time period between one year on Earth and one year on Planet X.

The number of gods on the assembly of council that ruled all was twelve.

They each were allotted their own sacred number: 5, 10, 15, 20, 25, 30, 35, 40, 45, 50, 55, 60. Each god had dedicated to them one planet of the solar system. The moon, the sun and Planet X included equals twelve in total. Each god had dedicated to them one month of the year to remind them of the number of planets in the system. Since Planet X was the most outer planet it was the seventh planet from Earth. If you were to travel direct to Planet X from Earth you would labour on past six planets and then take a rest at your destination, the seventh planet. To remind them of the distance between Earth and Planet X the week was divided into seven days with the seventh day being a day of rest. The seven gods with the highest numbers were given the distinction of being the seven who judge; this meant that they would meet more frequently on more pressing matters when it was not practical to assemble all twelve gods. To each of the seven who judge was dedicated one day of the week. When all discussion failed and no decision could be reached, ultimately the power to rule supreme was given to the god with highest number.

Each of the twelve gods on council was dedicated one zodiac constellation and one zodiac symbol as their own. This was most important because the number system for each god was allocated on a rotation basis with the power to rule supreme going to the god of the current zodiac age. When the zodiac would shift to a new age, the power to rule supreme would shift with it. To determine what zodiac age the Earth was in, the zodiac constellations were viewed through astronomical observatories. The gateway to a temple would be aligned to a solstice so that when that day came, the sun would shine directly through.

Using the temple gateway as your viewport, if you look out to the horizon on solstice day at break of dawn when the stars are still visible, the constellation directly above the sun will indicate the current zodiac. If you return to the same observatory at the same time the following year, the constellations will be seen to have shifted slightly in conjunction with the precession of the Earth.

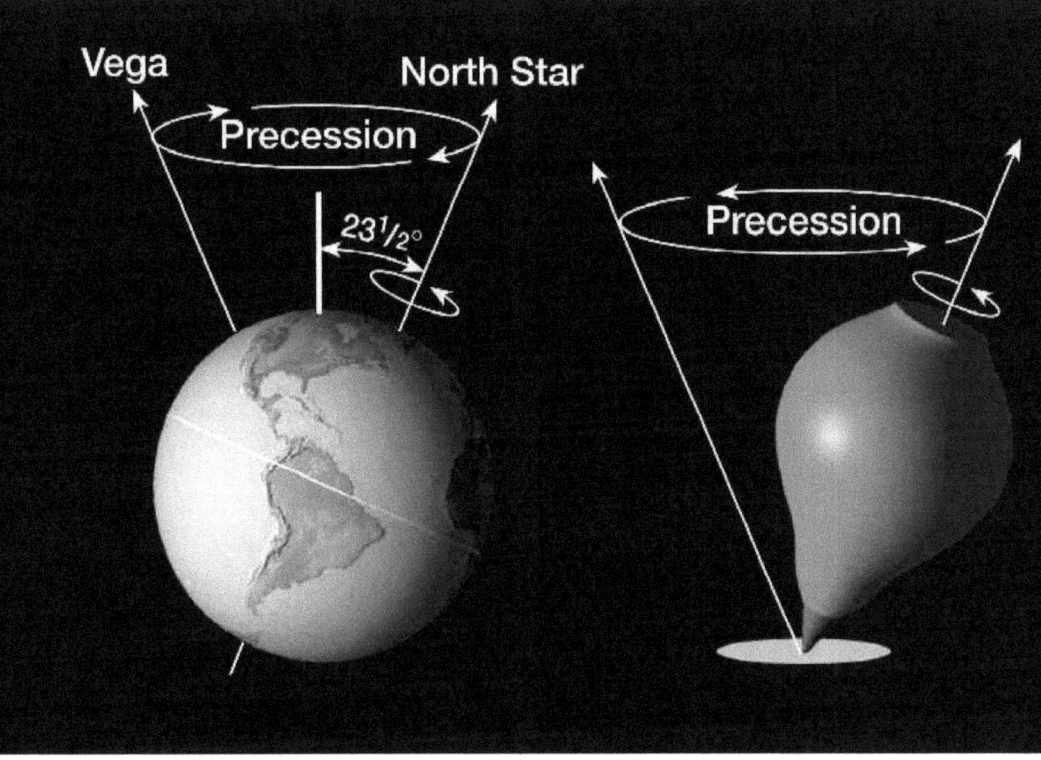

In 2,160 years Earth will have completed 30 degrees of its precessional cycle, bringing into your view port the dawning of a new zodiac age.

There is a simple way to observe, on a small scale, what the earth does on it's precessional cycle, by using a spinning top or a dreidel. When spinning a top or a dreidel you will notice that while they rotate, the centre axis will slowly wobble around in a circular motion. You can often place a finger within the circle without touching the axis. This wobble is exactly what the axis of the earth does on it's precessional cycle, on a much larger scale.

A dreidel is a very ancient toy used traditionally by Jewish people on festival days. A dreidel is made in the shape of a cube which has been partially cut out from a globe, with the bottom part still globular, and from the top protrudes the axis. Using a four-sided dreidel as a model for a revolving earth gives us the meaning for the term "the four corners of the globe".

One of the oldest depictions of the zodiacs ever found was discovered on the ceiling of the Hathor temple Dendera Egypt. The depictions here were showing exactly the same 12 zodiac symbols that we use in astrology today.

Some of the archaeologists estimated the age of the Dendera zodiac to be around 4,500 years old. This became a subject of debate, because to accept this meant that the Egyptians of antiquity had knowledge of the precession of the Earth. Many of the archaeologists argued that the Egyptians of 4,500 years ago only copied the symbols from the even older engraving of the Sumerians.

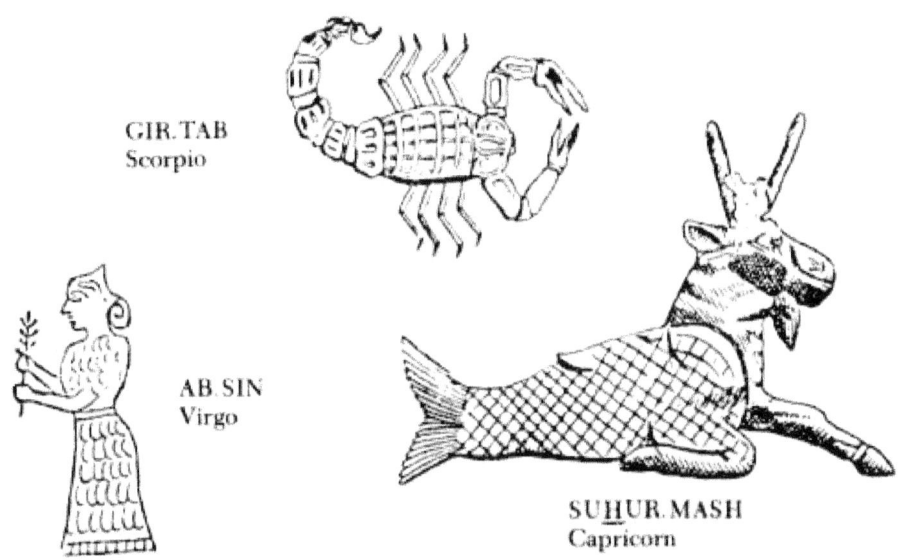

This seems to be quite an achievement for people from so long ago, considering that in 1615, the Romans placed Galileo Galilei under house arrest for the rest of his life for suggesting that the Earth orbited the sun. This does however raise another interesting question. If the Romans in 1615 did not know that the Earth orbited the Sun, how did they establish the calender, which had counted 1615 orbits around the sun since the birth of Christ? It must have been that it was easy for the Romans of that time to use the Jewish/Hebrew calendar and wind it back to zero so that they could call it their own. According to the Jewish/Hebrew calendar, the year 2014 is really the year 5774.

CHAPTER EIGHT:
Babylon, Sodom and Gomorrah

When 2,160 years had passed in the age of Taurus, it was expected that the power to rule supreme would be handed over to Aries by the "bull of heaven", the god Enlil. However, all the viewports were showing the Earth was still in Taurus. What had happened? Had the massive energy shift of the flood caused the retardation of the precession of the Earth so that the age of Taurus was started over again? This seemed okay for Taurus but for Aries they had decided that since their time to rule supreme was imminent they would wait no longer to take what was rightfully theirs. In defiance to the will of the gods, the greatest city of all was to be built: the new bond of Heaven and Earth, the gateway to the gods, Babylon.

A new situation had been created for which the gods were again called to assembly. For the first time humans were being rallied in support of a cause that was in opposition to the governing authority of gods. This was a real problem because if the Babylonians were able to gather enough human support they could cause a revolution strong enough to overpower the gods.

To prevent humans from being united against the gods it was decided that future settlements were to be taught to speak different languages. Civilisations were created independently and positioned over different parts of the world so they would not mingle with each other. In this way disunity among humans was guaranteed.

Genesis chapter 11:6, 7, 8.

And the Lord said, Behold the people is one, and they have all one language; and this they begin to do; and now nothing will be restrained from them, which they have imagined to do.

Go to, let us go down, and there confound their language, that they may not understand one another's speech.

So the Lord scattered them abroad from thence upon the face of all the earth …

The god of the star sign Aries already owned much land and had vast empires in Egypt, but his reason for claiming the location of Babylon on the Euphrates River was because this was the most central part of the civilised world of that time. A position fitting for the supreme ruler of the world. The problem this caused for Earth's colony was that Babylon had dammed the river and had diverted water through canals, causing a water shortage for the cities of Earth's colony located downstream.

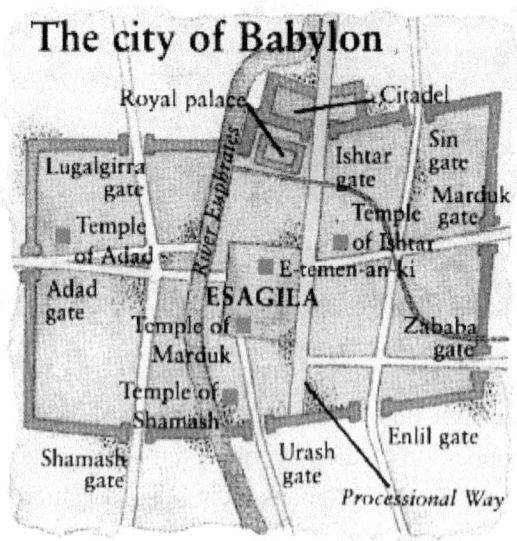

Creating disunity in the human race was a clever strategy to prevent the sudden growth of the Babylonians, but it did not prevent growth at their own pace. The empire of the Babylonians had been extended by building new cities at Sodom and Gomorrah. Again the operations of Earth's colony were being disrupted. The gods in council saw this as defiance to the wishes of the highest god, and so to restore their own operations to the fullest, the council decided to use force to stop the Babylonians and the sinning cities of Sodom and Gomorrah.

Genesis chapter 14:1, 2, 3.

And it came to pass in the days of Amraphel king of Shinar, Arioch king of Ellasar, Chedorlaomer king of Elam, and Tidal king of nations;

That these made war with Bera king of Sodom, and with Birsha king of Gomorrah, Shinab king of Admah, and Shemeber king of Zeboiim, and the king of Bela, which is Zoar.

All these were joined together in the vale of Siddim, which is the salt sea.

From Planet X awesome weapons had been kept in storage in caves high in mountains. Similar weapons had been exploded inside volcanoes on Planet X to try to increase the greenhouse effect. They were now kept if needed to blast an asteroid if ever one was seen as a threat. The fateful decision was made to use awesome weapons to obliterate the cities built without permission of the council, in order to fully restore the operations of the highest god.

Genesis chapter 14:20.

And blessed be the most high god ...

Weapons of this type had never before been used in warfare and so it was not known what the results of their use might be.

Genesis chapter 19:24, 28.

Then the Lord rained upon Sodom and upon Gomorrah brimstone and fire from the Lord out of heaven;

And he looked toward Sodom and Gomorrah, and toward all the land of the plain, and behold, and, the smoke of the country went up as the smoke of a furnace.

The cities of Sodom and Gomorrah were completely obliterated, the craters were so large the Salt Sea poured into them, completely removing any trace.

The target Babylon was never reached. It was not anticipated that the fallout created by the cloud of the blasts would kill all the life in the cities of Earth's colony. By a strange twist of fate the only city that remained unharmed was Babylon.

CHAPTER NINE:
The One God

Earth's colony in the land between the rivers Tigris and Euphrates was never rebuilt. The land was left unsafe and contaminated by the evil winds of the blasts. The fateful decision to exercise zero tolerance toward Babylon had cost the gods the entire civilisation of Earth's colony.

In Babylon, the god Marduk known by the star sign Aries, denied the divinity of any of the other gods. He glorified himself and declared that there shall be no other gods before him. Upon himself he bestowed the attributes of all the other gods. Monotheism - the belief in one God - was born.

The sacred scriptures were rewritten, where the one God bestowed upon himself the creation of the Heavens and the Earth. To himself he dedicated the mightiest in all of the solar system, Planet X. To his subjects he told of how out of all the gods it was he who split the Earth in two pieces, creating the Earth and the Heavens. The new scriptures were engraved on seven clay tablets. The first six told the story of creation by God while on the seventh tablet the god rested and announced the public holiday festivals to be held throughout the coming year. The seven tablets of creation are known by their opening words, which mean in English "when on high". In Babylonian they are called "Enuma-Ellish".

Enuma-Ellish - The Seven Tablets Of Creation

In other parts of the world gods were well-known, most famously in Egypt, Rome, Greece, Scandinavia, Asia, India, and South America.

It was approximately the year 1600, during the age of Aries that Planet X made its most recent approach towards Earth. It was then that the gods gave one last gift to mankind. Humans on Earth were granted the gift of freedom from the gods. By this time Earth was vastly civilised and the affairs of humans dominated the land, taking precedence over the affairs of the gods. The gods were increasingly becoming aloof the more and more the population of humans increased. With Planet X approaching and the Earth colony now ended, the gods had decided to return home and to leave earth under the leadership of the kings and the Holy Grail. The sacred royal bloodline was chosen to rule Earth in place of the gods, effectively upgrading the status of the human race as a whole.

When the time had come for the gods to depart, a promise was made that one day the gods would return for all of their people who loved them. Before then at the end of the age of Aries a new king would be born to rule supreme on the council of twelve, like the highest god. His spirit would live on to guide people through the next zodiac age. The symbol dedicated to him was the symbol for the next zodiac.

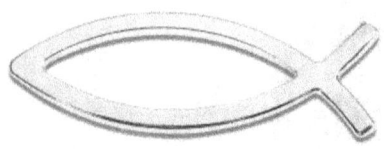

CHAPTER TEN:
A Universal Language

At the time of leaving Earth the gods were satisfied that the world was left in the capable hands of the chosen kings. The gods would always do their best to look after their people - after all, they saw themselves as the shepherds of the human race. For the gods to declare their love for the human race, some sort of communication was needed. The kings could be entrusted to deliver the message but how well this was done depended on how clever the kings were. Communicating messages by word of mouth could eventually be forgotten with time. Scripting the message on clay tablets and archiving them in temple libraries was not going to reach most people. The value of scripts was limited to people who had special knowledge of what they meant. People with no literacy skills or who spoke different languages could not comprehend them. When the situation required it the gods had a method of communication that would deliver the message direct to all people throughout time. To convey a message that was universal and could be understood by people of all languages and all classes of society, the use of symbolism was employed. The use of symbolic hieroglyphs or pictographs by ancient people is in principle no different to today's use of computer icons or road signs. At a glance, a picture can convey a thousand words.

If read correctly, a recurring symbol throughout history holds the key to understanding the promise of the gods.

The meaning of the symbolism of the serpents coiled around a rod, which was used by the original Sumerian Earth colony, can be read like this: of all the creatures of Earth, the serpent is the most Earth-hugging and is literally closest to the Earth. For that reason it is shown here as a representation of all creatures of Earth. The rod represents the shepherd's crook, reminiscent of the beginning when the gods nurtured and bred the human race themselves like the good shepherd nurtures and breeds his sheep. The wings are the wings of angels shown here to represent the divine intervention by the gods. Together the symbols represent the promise that the gods will be there always to nurture and love the human race. The symbolism was reused thousands of years later by the Roman god Mercury, and in the design of the Caduceus of the god Hermes.

The Greek god Asclepius used the symbol of a serpent coiled around a pole for healing and the same symbol today is used by medical organisations around the world.

In the Bible Moses used a brass snake coiled around a pole to deliver to people divine healing. This symbol is widely compared for its similarity to the symbol of Jesus on the cross.

This symbolism was used by the Roman sun god Mithras. And in more recent times, some of the Mithraic symbolism was used again in the design of the No. 21 world tarot card that features the earth goddess, Gaea.

Additional symbolism in a rock carving of the god Mithras shows the god with the sun radiating from behind his head while his right hand holds the torch of illumination for his people. The same symbolism was used again thousands of years later, by the statue in New York harbour of the Roman goddess Libertas.

Carrying on today the tradition of the shepherd's crook with the coiled serpents, are the bishops in different organisations around the world.

The Pope uses all of his attire to make it obvious to people that he is carrying the staff representing the love of the good shepherd.

In 2013 the symbol of entwined serpents was commemorated worldwide with special edition coins celebrating the Year of the Snake.

CHAPTER ELEVEN:
What's in a Name?

In the ancient world it was common practise for high profile people to include the name of their god in their own name. Some well-known examples of this tradition are shown by the ancient Egyptians. The name of the pharoah Tutankhamen has the suffix dedicating the pharoah to the Egyptian god Amen. The word "ankh" was the Egyptian word meaning life. It was depicted by its hieroglyphic symbol and can be seen in statues in the hand of the god himself. The ankh symbol is often seen in pictographs together with the celestial globe Aten as it extends life.

In full, the name Tutankhamen means, "living image of the god Amen". The name of the god could be included as either a suffix or a prefix. Likewise, the name of the Egyptian pharoah Ramesses has the prefix Ra, dedicating him to the god Ra. In full the name Ramesses means, "Ra bore him".

According to the Sumerian legends, the god who ruled supreme during the age of Taurus at the time of the flood was called the Lord of the Command, and his name was Enlil. At that time there was no absolute spelling or pronunciation for a word or name, so the Sumerian god Enlil was known to the Babylonians as Ellil and to the Canaanites simply as El. An ancient stela found in Palestine shows the Canaanite god El seated in typical Sumerian fashion wearing a horned headdress, and is depicted with the winged globe above his head.

The Canaanites are known to us early in the Bible as the decendents of the grandson of Noah, from Genesis chapter 9:18, 19, 10:6,15, 19, 20.

> And the sons of Noah that went forth of the ark, were Shem, and Ham, and Japheth; and Ham is the father of Canaan.
>
> These are the three sons of Noah; and of them was the whole earth overspread.
>
> And the sons of Ham; Cush and Mizraim, and Phut, and Canaan.
>
> And Canaan begat Sidon his firstborn and Heth.
>
> And the border of the Canaanites was from Sidon, as thou comest to Gerar, unto Gaza; as thou goest, unto Sodom, and Gomorrah, and Admah, and Zeboim, even unto Lasha.
>
> These are the sons of Ham, after their families, after their tongues, in their countries, and in their nations.

It is undoubtable from these references that the nation of the Canaanites that worshipped El, were descended from Canaan, the grandson of the flood-hero Noah, who was chosen by god in Genesis chapter 6:8, 9.

But Noah found grace in the eyes of the Lord.

These are the generations of Noah: Noah was a just man and perfect in his generations, and Noah walked with god.

It does seem remarkable that the nation of the Canaanites, so closely related to the chosen Noah, was so quickly worshipping another deity. A clue to solving this mystery could be provided to us in the Book of Genesis chapter 9:20, 21, 22, 23, 24, 25, 26, 27.

And Noah began to be an husbandman, and he planted a vineyard:

And he drank of the wine, and was drunken; and he was uncovered within his tent.

And Ham the father of Canaan, saw the nakedness of his father, and told his two brethren without.

And Shem and Japheth took a garment, and laid it upon both their shoulders, and went backward, and covered the nakedness of their father; and their faces were backward, and they saw not their father's nakedness.

And Noah awoke from his wine, and knew what his younger son had done unto him.

And he said, Cursed be Canaan; a servant of servants shall he be unto his brethren.

And he said, Blessed be the Lord God of Shem: and Canaan shall be his servant.

God shall enlarge Japheth, and he shall dwell in the tents of Shem; and Canaan shall be his servant.

In this section of the Bible, the "just" Noah chosen by god, had decided to curse and punish Canaan, the son of Ham, for something Ham had done in advertantly. Perhaps this was a good reason for the Canaanites changing deities.

According to the Sumerian tradition, the highest god at the time of the deluge was named Enlil, and is the same as the god El worshipped by the

Canaanites. As a grandson of Noah, and Noah was chosen by god, that made Canaan himself a chosen one.

So, did Canaan change gods, or was the god of the Book of Genesis really Enlil/El? The writers of the Bible did not give a name to their god, so we must assume that they are two different deities.

Despite the apparent difference in deities, the tradition of using the name of the god El for either the prefix or the suffix in a name is widely seen throughout the Bible and is still carried on throughout the world today. Many people today choose to give their children a biblical name containing the name of the god El. For example, the name Michael is in common use today and it carries the meaning "who is like god?", literally "who is like (the god of the Canaanites) El?". The bible is full of examples of names that either end or start in this fashion. Some of these are Gabriel, Daniel, Samuel, Joel, Nathaniel, Ezekiel, Israel, Ishmael, Rachel, Jezebel, or Elijah, Elisha, and so on. All of these names carry a meaning that can be traced back to their association with the god of the Sumerians, Enlil.

Another interesting usage of the name of a god as either the suffix or prefix for a name, can be seen in the use of the name of the god Ea. Known to the Sumerians as Lord of Earth, his name was carried forward as a suffix, used in the name of the Earth god from the Greek pantheon, Gaea. Today the name of the god Ea is a prefix for the name of planet Earth.

The Canaanites being closely related to a biblical patriarch and worshipping a different god is not an isolated incidence in the Bible. In Genesis chapter 19:36, 37 we are told that Lot, the nephew of the patriarch Abraham, had a son called Moab who went on to become the father to the nation of Moabites.

> Thus were both the daughters of Lot with child by their father.

> And the firstborn bare a son, and called his name Moab; the same is the father of the Moabites unto this day.

We now know from discoveries made in the ruins of the ancient city of Moab that the Moabites were the worshippers of the goddess Ashtar-Chemosh. This should hardly be surprising at this stage since we also know that Abraham hails from the city of the Sumerian moon god Nanna/Sin. We know that the Canaanites, descended from the grandson of Noah, worshipped the god El, so now we can see a pattern emerging. It seems that God had a dilemma in trying to get people to be loyal to the one god. This does explain why later on in the Bible, in the commandments that God engraved and gave to Moses atop Mount Sinai, the first laws were -

Exodus chapter 20:2,3,4,5.

I am the Lord thy God, Thou shalt have no other gods before me.

Thou shalt not make unto thee any graven image, or any likeness of anything that is in heaven above,

Thou shalt not bow down thyself to them, nor serve them: for I the Lord thy God am a jealous God.

In this passage, God's reference to himself as a jealous God, does imply that he was not the only god. Also, if God was such a jealous god, why then did he give the name Israel to Jacob the grandson of Abraham?

Genesis chapter 32:24, 28.

And Jacob was left alone; and there wrestled a man with him until the breaking of day.

And he said, Thy name shall be called no more Jacob, but Israel: for as a prince hast thou power with God and with men, and hast prevailed.

In this passage it is explained by God that the name Israel actually means, "the one who wrestled and prevailed with God". Again, the suffix El meaning god, refers back to the name of the god of the Canaanites, El. So, why does a jealous God give the name of a rival god to one of his subjects? It could be that since the god in the Bible did not give his name, then the writers of the Bible used the name of the next closest thing to refer to God, and that was the name of the god El.

The shortage of a name for God, and the substitution with the next closest name, can be seen at different times throughout history. When Jesus gave the Lord's prayer to his disciples, at the sermon on the mount, the prayer finished with the name of the Egyptian god Amen.

Matthew chapter 6:13.

And lead us not into temptation, but deliver us from evil: For thine is the kingdom, and the power, and the glory, forever, Amen.

Invoking the name of the god Amen at the end of a prayer, was standard practice for ancient Egyptians. This could easily have been taught to Jesus in his early life in Egypt. In Matthew 2:13, an angel of the Lord commands Joseph, Mary, and baby Jesus to flee to Egypt, to escape from king Herod. At the time of the sermon on the mount, the Jewish custom would not have allowed any person to speak the name of the god Jehovah, so Jesus would have chosen the next closest name, and the prayer ended in typical Egyptian fashion, invoking the god Amen.

Another instance of substituting the name of another god, for the God in the bible has been shown by the Romans. When the Romans of 313AD decided to become Christian, they had no name for God the Father that Jesus spoke of. God the Father to the Romans was called Jupiter. Jupiter is acknowledged today as being the same as Dyeus Piter the chief deity of the prehistoric Proto-Indo-European societies, and Zeus as God the Father of the Greek pantheon.

In the final translation in the Latin vulgate Bible, the resulting word for God was a mixture of the names of all three gods and became Deus. Also in the Latin vulgate Bible is a list of Bible names starting with the name of the god El, shown next to their meaning in latin which starts with the word Deus, or Dei, meaning god.

DE MUNDI CREATIONE, RERUM
& ornatu; deque hominis formatione, cui

IN ‡ principio creavit Deus cælum, & terram.
2. Terra autem erat inanis & vacua, & tenebræ erant ſuper faciem abyſſi: & ſpiritus Dei ferebatur ſuper aquas.
3. Dixitque Deus: || Fiat lux. Et facta eſt lux.
4. Et vidit Deus lucem quòd eſſet bona: & diviſit lucem à tenebris.
5. Appellavitque lucem Diem, & tenebras

Deus zelotes.
Eleazar, Dei adjutorium.
Elchanan, Dei gratia ſive miſericor
Eliacim, Dei reſurrectio.
Elias, Deus Dominus.
Eliezer, Dei adjutorium.
Elimelech, Deus meus rex.
Eliſabeth, Deus juramenti

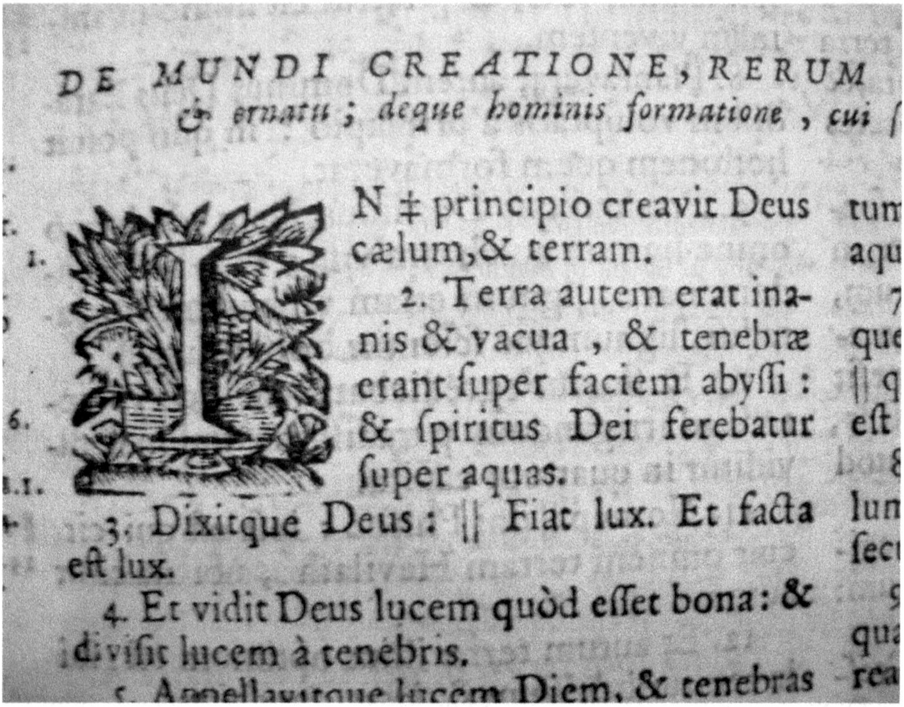

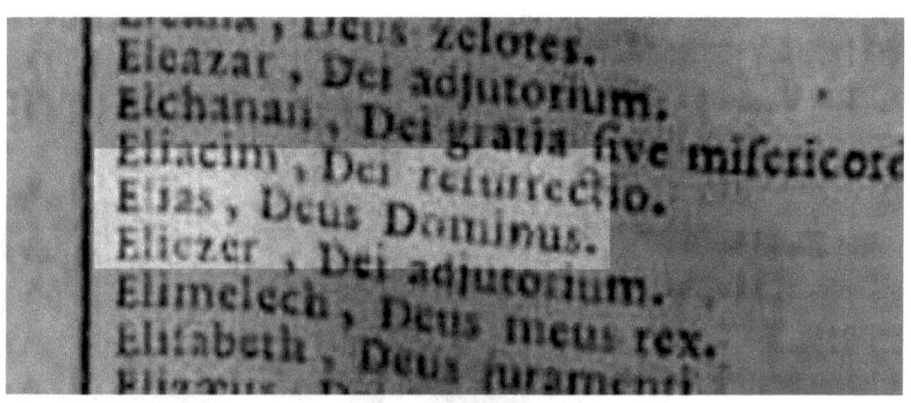

Some English renderings of the word Deus are deity, diva, divine, divination, theism, and atheist. A Roman statue depicting Archangel Michael slaying Satan, represented as a dragon, has the Latin words engraved on his shield “Quis Ut Deus?” meaning “Who is like God?”.

In the Bible, the only indication for the name of God is given to us when God identifies himself to Moses in Exodus 3:14.

> And God said unto Moses, I AM WHO I AM: and he said, Thus shalt thou say unto the children of Israel, I AM hath sent me unto you.

Taking into account the many discepancies for the identity of God, there is still one way that we can unzip an answer to this mystery. If we use God's own description of himself, "I am who I am", and we extend the phrase to fit the context of our story so it says; "I am, who I am at the time", then, we no longer have any discrepancy.

The practise of naming a king or queen with a name that relates them to their god was widely practised in the ancient world in places like Egypt, Sumeria, Assyria, and can still be seen in the world today. In the Bible, the Assyrian king Asenappar (Ezra 4;10), is known to us today as Ashurbanipal. His name dedicates him to the god Ashur and means "Ashur is creator of an heir". Today the name of Elizabeth the Queen of England, is an English rendering for the Hebrew name "Elisheba" and means "God's promise". In the 21st century, the name of the future king William has the meaning "the protector". The name William derives from the German name Wilhelm, which has the last four letters "helm", short for helmet, hence the meaning "protector". Unlike it's German counterpart, William is spelt with the last three letters "iam", which in the bible was the only name given for God, by God himself in Exodus 3:14.

> Thus shalt thou say unto the children of Israel, I AM hath sent me unto you.

The change in the spelling of the name alters the meaning from its original German so that the meaning of William can now be read as "will of God".

CHAPTER TWELVE:
Some Questions Answered by the Stars

Does observing the orbit of the Earth today enable us to predict where Earth is headed in the future? The answer is yes. In the first chapter of this book we looked at two possibilities linking the origin of Earth to the sun; there is also a third clue. The orbit of Earth around the sun is circular and, ever so slightly, Earth is slowly moving away from the sun. This is important because Earth is not simply being drawn into the sun, caught in its gravitational field. Earth has enough of its own momentum to keep pulling away from the sun to continue travelling further into space. In effect, the orbit of Earth is circular with a slight outward spiral that continually increases the diameter of the circle of orbit.

From where did the Earth gain its momentum? The most plausible answer to this is from the sun itself. If Earth was originally a piece of the sun that was ejected into space with enough momentum to never return, it would do exactly what it is doing now - orbit with a slow outward spiral. If we consider that today Earth's orbit is taking it away from the sun, then we must know from this that in the past Earth was closer to the sun. If we were to trace backwards through time the path of Earth's orbit, with it continually spiralling inwards towards the sun, it would eventually lead us to its origin, the sun.

This same process of expulsion of matter from the sun into space, creating a planet with enough momentum to gain an outward spiralling orbit, was the same process that created all of the planets located in the ecliptic plane. The first planet to be created would have been Neptune. Millions of years later while Neptune slowly spiralled out into space, the sun created Uranus. While Neptune and Uranus continued on their slowly spiralling orbit out into space, the sun created Saturn. In the first chapter of this book Saturn is listed as being created with a satellite called Pluto. When Planet X first passed through our solar system, its gravitational pull attracted Pluto away from Saturn and locked it into its own solar orbit that was at an incline to the ecliptic plane, like Planet X.

While Saturn slowly spiralled out into space, the sun created Jupiter, and so on until today when the youngest of all the planets is Mercury.

Millions of years into the future, the planets of our solar system will have spiralled so far out into space that they could become attracted by the gravitational field of other solar systems and become lost in space, like the planet that became lost in our solar system, Planet X. A planet such as Neptune that today is incapable of supporting life, could venture into another star system, collide into another planet, gain the seed of life, and become a civilised and hospitable planet. This is also a possible future for all of the planets in our solar system.

The Earth is today orbiting in what is called the habitable zone. This means that it is the right distance away from the sun so that it is not too cold or too hot, and can sustain life. What will happen eventually when the Earth's outward spiralling orbit brings it out of the habitable zone? This means that all life on Earth may eventually become extinct. This would be a very slow process and certainly wouldn't happen for millions of years into the future.

How can we save ourselves from becoming extinct by venturing too far out into space? While Earth is moving out of the habitable zone, the outward spiralling orbit of Venus will bring Venus into the habitable zone.

On Venus, what are at the moment poisonous gases will undergo chemical changes as the planet cools on its journey away from the sun. These gases will solidify, leaving an atmosphere that will be much more hospitable to life. At this time it will make sense for people of the Earth to start planet-hopping from Earth to Venus, so that they can spread the seed of life from a fertile planet like Earth to a completely virgin planet like Venus.

As Earth becomes more inhospitable Venus might eventually take over all life from Earth.

Millions of years after this, while Venus is moving out of the habitable zone, it will make sense to planet-hop again to Mercury. Hopefully, before Mercury's outward spiralling orbit brings it out of the habitable zone, the sun will have given birth to more planets.

When will the gods from Planet X return to Earth? One of the things we should take into account is that the last time Planet X returned near Earth all of the gods left with a promise to return at an undetermined time in the future. The previous time all of the gods left Earth was just prior to the deluge. At that time they did not give a warning of what was to come, but nonetheless by command of the Creator of All they were there to save the seed of life from Earth. If there is to be a catastrophe in the future large enough to wipe out the whole Earth, the likelihood is that the gods will then return from Planet X to save again the seed of life from Earth.

The return of the gods will have to be before the impending catastrophe if they are to arrive in time to save people. How will the people of today greet the visitors from Planet X if they are to return? What type of people will believe and ascend to the heavens with them? The people most likely to be available to leave Earth will be the ones who own the least and have nothing to lose. The people who have accumulated the most material wealth here on Earth will most likely wish to remain here with their possessions. Maybe after Earth has been destroyed and then renewed the day will come that the meek will inherit the Earth.

The last time a catastrophic event such as the end of the Ice Age occurred was during the age of Taurus, so it is probable that this scenario will not happen again for another nine ages of the zodiac. This makes it very interesting to examine the possibility; however, it is unlikely to have any real effect on our lives today.

Is there anything major likely to happen in the near future during our own lifetime? The answer again is yes. The most likely significant event of the near future is the dawning of the Age of Aquarius.

With this transition we can expect the rule of the One God Supreme to change from the Fish to the Cup Bearer.

Approximately 2014 years ago three wise men observed the stars had changed to Pisces and so predicted the time had arrived for the birth of a new messiah.

If we wish to be wise we also can look at the stars for the dawning of the Age of Aquarius to predict the coming of a new messiah. Of course, a strange bright star in the sky would help.

Bibliography

Albert Silotti, Pyramids of Egypt.

White Star 1997.

Arthur Cotterell General Editor, The Encyclopedia of World Mythology. Dempsey Parr 1999.

Authorized King James Version, The Holy Bible.

The National Publishing Co. 1975.

Erich von Daniken, Chariots of the Gods.

Souvenir Press Ltd. 1969.

Erich von Daniken, Return to the Stars.

Souvenir Press Ltd. 1970.

Erich von Daniken, The Gold of the Gods.

Souvenir Press Ltd. 1973.

Gae Callender, The Eye of Horus.

Longman Cheshire Pty Ltd. 1993.

George J. Haas and William R. Saunders,

The Cydonia Codex. Frog Ltd. 2005.

George J. Haas and William R. Saunders,
The Martian Codex. North Atlantic Books 2009.

Graeme Whittle, Alchemy: The Quest for the Philosopher's Stone. Crawford House Press 1993.

Ian Wilson, Jesus the Evidence.
Pan Books Ltd. 1985.

Laurence Gardner, Bloodline of the Holy Grail.
Element Books Ltd. 1996.

Laurence Gardner, Genesis of the Grail Kings.
Transworld Publishers 1999.

Laurence Gardner, Realm of the Ring Lords.
Fair Winds Press 2000.

Laurence Gardner, Lost Secrets of the Sacred Ark.
Element Books Ltd. 2003.

Laurence Gardner, The Shadow of Solomon.
Element Books Ltd. 2005.

Laurence Gardner, The Grail Enigma.
Element Books Ltd. 2008.

Noel Streatfeild, The Boy Pharoah Tutankhamen.
Michael Joseph Ltd. 1972.

Peter Partner, The Story of Christianity.
ABC Books 2006.

Reader's Digest, Vanished Civilisations.
Reader's Digest Services Pty. Ltd. 1983.

Thomas Paine, The Age of Reason.
G.P. Putnam's Sons 1896.

Zecharia Sitchin, The 12th Planet.
Avon Books 1978.

Zecharia Sitchin, The Stairway to Heaven.
Avon Books 1983.

Zecharia Sitchin, The Wars of Gods and Men.
Avon Books 1985.

Zecharia Sitchin, The Lost Realms. Harper 1990.

Zecharia Sitchin, When Time Began. Harper 1993.

Zecharia Sitchin, Divine Encounters. Avon Books 1995.

Zecharia Sitchin, The Cosmic Code. Harper 1998.

Zecharia Sitchin, The Lost Book of Enki. Bear & Company 2002.

Zecharia Sitchin, There Were Giants Upon the Earth. Bear & Company 2010.

Images supplied by flickr.com

Engraving of title page by Lucio Licciardello.